How to (Hu)MAN UP in Modern Society

How to (Hu)MAN UP in Modern Society

HEAL YOURSELF & SAVE THE WORLD

LOGAN COHEN

gatekeeper press
Columbus, Ohio

How to (Hu)Man Up in Modern Society: Heal Yourself & Save the World

Published by Gatekeeper Press
2167 Stringtown Rd, Suite 109
Columbus, OH 43123-2989
www.GatekeeperPress.com

Library of Congress Control Number: 2021938383

ISBN (hardcover): 9781662911316
ISBN (paperback): 9781662911323
eISBN: 9781662911330

CONTENTS

DEDICATION

It was only after my grandfather's death that I learned he was rescued from the concentration camps by Oscar Schindler, a German citizen who was the focus of an Emmy Award-winning movie in 1994 called *Schindler's List*.[1] He rarely spoke of daily life during the Holocaust, but there were plenty of stories about growing up on a small farm in Poland during the 1930s while the political tension mounted, leading up to both of his parents and six of his seven siblings being killed in the concentration camps by Hitler and the Nazis.

I grew up on the same street as my grandfather "Sam"— six houses down the road to be exact—where my own family lived in Atlanta, Georgia. The Jewish household where I was raised looked warm and inviting from the outside, but inside was unpredictable and sometimes unsafe. There were many days that I would avoid going directly home after the walk back from school; instead, stopping at my grandfather's house to spend as much time as possible. At first, this daily stop at my grandfather's house was for the sole purpose of avoiding the chaos of my home life. As I grew older and we became more comfortable with each other personally, the stories of World War II, surviving the Holocaust, and beginning his life in America began to flow more readily.

We talked about other things of course—his German shepherd "Rex" that was the trusted breed of the Nazis due to their combination of fierceness and intelligence; his love of the Oprah Winfrey Show as a sign that like him, people can overcome the odds by surviving horrible conditions to thrive;

---

1   *An Amblin Entertainment production. (1994). Schindler's list. Universal City, Calif.: MCA Universal Home Video.*

and last, but not least, the importance of community service. The last topic of community service was rarely one of direct conversation but was modeled each time we went on one of our frequent outings in downtown Atlanta.

Atlanta, Georgia, was an interesting place to grow up in the 1980s and 1990s. The city's population exploded after the completion of an international airport in 1980, but the crack-cocaine epidemic hit Atlanta hard, and the homeless population became notorious for a persistent—even aggressive style of panhandling that made tourists and even some locals nervous. Sam never blinked an eye when he was the target of a hostile approach by a panhandler. He knew they were hungry and as a Holocaust Survivor who almost starved to death on a few occasions himself, he could only feel compassion for these malnourished human beings.

Sam would never avoid them in the streets, no matter how dirty they happened to be or how aggressively they would beg, and would always listen to their stories until there was a pause where he could ask, "Are you hungry?" I never heard anyone say "No."

From there, we would all walk together to a local restaurant, where Sam would approach the cashier to instruct them to take the homeless person's order and prepare whatever food was requested. At this point Sam would pay the tab, then he and I would continue on our planned outing in the city.

I soaked up these stories of grit and unending determination from the Holocaust, as well as the personal experiences of watching Sam serve the vulnerable members of his community with compassion and humanity. I didn't realize it at the time, but these experiences would become invaluable as an adult—even forming the foundation for a natural sense of the intimate connections between freedom, accountability, love, resilience, and community.

I come to you not only as the author of this book but also as the grandson of a Holocaust survivor, and a man whose life has been made possible—both directly and indirectly—by a German citizen and registered member of the Nazi party named Oscar Schindler who broke free from the political brainwashing of his time. There are occasions in life where it is very difficult to figure out the "right thing" to do. Sometimes, there is even a heavy price to pay for doing the "right thing," which can make this *right thing* seem like a relatively heavy burden to carry. But I want you to come to personally understand that even in the face of the greatest adversity and oppression, the power of love can still prevail over the love of power.

Loss, pain, and violence are scary and extremely painful in their own right. These are powerful experiences and I would never intentionally minimize them or diminish the cost involved in coping with them. With that being said, I beg of you to *refuse* to let your fear and/or the love of power win. Instead, by doing the *right thing* out of the power of love—rather than the love of power—we can heal ourselves in this lifetime, as well as empower the lives of many other community members—some who we might not even know personally. Some of these people, myself included at the time of Oscar Schindler's famous deeds of goodwill, might not have even been born yet!

Beyond material success and winning in competition, this is how a person creates a true legacy—a legend that will live on forever. Because while heroes are remembered, legends never die.

This one is for you, Mr. Schindler.

CHAPTER 1: PURPOSE AS THE KEY TO HEALTH, HAPPINESS & SUCCESS

As the grandson of an Auschwitz survivor who was on *Schindler's List*, I found it intuitive that serving our more vulnerable community members is a process that very literally creates life and healing for both parties. I grew up with firsthand stories of gritty survival through community effort in the concentration camps. Then later, as a young boy, I watched examples of my grandfather continuing to embody these same values. As an adult, I came to understand the confusion in Oscar Schindler's voice during interviews as he received praise and adoration for his rescue efforts after World War II, repeatedly coming back to the phrase, "I should have saved more. I could have saved more…"

In many ways, a mere 1,200 Jews saved compared to the 6,000,000 Jews killed is a drop in the bucket. At only 0.02% of the total number killed, it can seem barely noteworthy in the face of that much annihilation. But it made a difference to my grandfather, and in the end, gave him a chance to empower himself to live a full life and start a family. Now as you read these words, I get to be here telling you about it. It is my only hope that this will in turn light a fire in your own heart and mind to start on this sacred journey of leadership by serving our community with whatever it is you have to offer.

This book is about "human empowerment"—teaching people to fish so they may continue serving their community for generations to come—and how it relates to "service"—an intentional act of generosity that empowers those served. This is opposed to "servitude," whereby you create a relationship of dependency by giving people resources until they rely on handouts, also known as "enabling." Even in the face of unspeakable pain and evil, every bit of service we do makes a difference in this life and the next. This is where the power of love will win against the love of power *every time.*

While growing up in a Jewish family in Atlanta, Georgia—a hustling metropolitan area nestled in the heart of the Deep South—I was also familiar with the practices and narratives of the Evangelical Christian community. I heard the stories of Jesus Christ being reborn and quickly observed the similarities of a life dedicated to service as practicing the power of love in a world that has become obsessed with the love of power—as both Jesus Christ and Buddha did—and the resulting healing for both the servant and community members served through this process as being central to Evangelical values.

Along my own life journey, first as a public servant in wilderness therapy settings with at-risk youth, and later working in community mental health, I developed a personal mission statement to aid in difficult decision-making when there was no "perfect solution," but I also had a responsibility to make the best decision possible for the people I was serving. Somewhere along the way, the phrase "What would Schindler do?" became my own means of evaluating personal decision-making to make sure I was serving adequately in a way that empowered others and at least avoided active participation in doing harm.

The knowledge that healing comes out of serving our community is an old one not only in faith-based settings, but also for the evolution of human beings as a species. The communities of our ancestors have enjoyed grassroots involvement with their tribes and communities for hundreds of thousands of years throughout the evolution of humankind.

Every person had an important role that was valued and interdependently woven into the daily rhythms of community life from our early beginnings as nomadic hunter/gatherer communities. It was not until the Industrial Revolution began only 250 years ago that human beings started a transition into a more global and interconnected community now characteristic of modern society, where traditional roles are now under pressure to evolve with the changing times.

Modern infrastructure can seem attractive and convenient, but this has in many ways separated human beings from experiencing an authentic level of personal value—or *purpose*—as a meaningful community member participating in urban life now driven by corporate interests, rather than human values.

In modern times, people must now create their *own* sense of purpose in life that is separate from the more rigid interpretation of traditional roles commonly used to measure personal success and happiness. Many people get caught up in self-identification with their job, the car they drive or the clothes they wear as markers of social prestige or personal success. However, these are merely material things that have very little bearing on quality of life.

Instead, a life driven by our own *unique* purpose—intentionally using our gifts and passions through decision-making driven by our core values shared meaningfully with others in important relationships—not only makes people happier and more productive, but also *physically healthier*. This dynamic balance is health promoting because it stimulates the "parasympathetic nervous system," the body's natural tool for healing and recovery.

The *parasympathetic nervous system* cannot be seen by the naked eye, but it is silently responsible for organizing the body's natural healing properties, also called "rest, recover, and digest," while the "sympathetic nervous system" rings the alarm bells for survival of an immediate threat, also called "fight, flight or freeze." These two systems of the body work off of each other to prioritize how energy will be used by the body. The fight/flight/freeze response of the body's sympathetic nervous system gets the blood pumping *out* of our major organs and into our arms and legs to maximize energy for surviving an immediate threat (i.e. fighting, running or "playing dead"), while the rest/recover/digest response of the parasympathetic nervous system brings blood flow back into our major organs so the available nutrients can promote healing, recovery, and critical thought.

Most people have an idea of the fight/flight/freeze response characteristic of panic or outrage of the *sympathetic nervous system*, but the relaxation and healing function of the *parasympathetic nervous system* is usually not as obvious. Even so, this state of relaxation for our nervous system is essential for *all* of the central healing systems of the body and without it, people literally fall apart on a very physical level. Symptoms of poor sympathetic response include suffering from chronic high blood pressure that puts more "wear and tear" on the heart (men are already three times more likely to have cardiovascular disease), disruption of immune function (even making it attack *itself* with "autoimmune disease"), poor digestion and gut health that blocks needed nutrient absorption,[2] poor critical thinking skills and even faster aging.[3]

---

2   McCorry L. K. (2007). Physiology of the autonomic nervous system. *American Journal of Pharmaceutical Education*, *71*(4), 78. https://doi.org/10.5688/aj710478

3   Lavretsky, H., and Newhouse, P. A. (2012). Stress, inflammation, and aging. *The American Journal of Geriatric Psychiatry : Official Journal of the American Association for Geriatric Psychiatry*, *20*(9), 729–733. https://doi.org/10.1097/JGP.0b013e31826573cf

There are many different chemicals that interact with each other to make these shifts occur to meet the demands of our immediate environment, but perhaps the most notable chemical involved is the stress hormone "cortisol" that is spilled into our bloodstream in bulk during the fight/flight/freeze response known as the sympathetic nervous system. Cortisol is a naturally occurring chemical as part of the normal stress response of the human body. When there is *too* much of it as the result of an *ongoing* stress response, as is quite typical of the overstimulation found in modern society, these unchecked levels of stress hormone will wreak havoc on the body and mind! Studies have shown clear connections between elevated levels of cortisol and faster aging, as well as lower testosterone levels that result in lower confidence and self-esteem, a decrease in physical strength, and lowered "serotonin" associated with depression and anxiety symptoms—even killing sex drive.[4]

If an accelerated aging process didn't catch your attention, that last sentence probably did! You are probably also wondering: *"How did the human body and mind get wired like this? And how can I use these natural forces, rather than let it to wear me down?"*

This may not come as a surprise, but the human body has *always* been this way since our early ancestors left the trees of the forest to compete against powerful predators at the top of the food chain. Human beings became successful because of our ability to solve problems dynamically as a community, meaning the more diversity that exists in our ranks, the more complicated problems a given group is capable of solving to secure mastery

---

4   Conradt, E., Abar, B., Lester, B. M., LaGasse, L. L., Shankaran, S., Bada, H., Bauer, C. R., Whitaker, T. M., and Hammond, J. A. (2014). Cortisol reactivity to social stress as a mediator of early adversity on risk and adaptive outcomes. *Child Development*, 85(6), 2279–2298. https://doi.org/10.1111/cdev.12316

over the environment.[5] This power of group collaboration is evident in most of the major human feats through history, whether hunting mastodons to successfully access enormous amounts of meat for our tribe, building pyramids that have stood the test of time, or landing on the moon. The use of group efforts to successfully manage our environment and *thrive* is what human beings do!

Research studies have also shown clear links between higher levels of compliance for individual community members when they have a *shared/community-driven* sense of purpose for task completion, rather than a more individual focus. A study in a hospital setting in 2007 showed that staff were more likely to complete health-promoting tasks when behaviors had the goal of avoiding negative consequences for a patient, rather than their *own* well-being. When hospital workers were asked to wash their hands for their own sanitation and protection, there were poor outcomes for compliance, but when hospital workers were asked to wash hands to protect *patients*, there was a 45% increase in compliance with safety measures.[6]

That statistic might seem surprising at first, that people are naturally more driven to look out for the well-being of other community members before their own. However, this has always been a part of human programming since our early ancestors relied on community-driven goals to survive. We are literally *programmed* on a biological level to "feel good/satisfied/motivated" to look out for our affiliated community

5   Naeem, S., Chazdon, R., Duffy, J. E., Prager, C., and Worm, B. (2016). Biodiversity and human well-being: an essential link for sustainable development. *Proceedings. Biological Sciences*, 283(1844), 20162091. https://doi.org/10.1098/rspb.2016.2091

6   Shigayeva, A., Green, K., Raboud, J.M. (2007). Factors associated with critical-care healthcare workers' adherence to recommended barrier precautions during the Toronto severe acute respiratory syndrome outbreak. *Infectious Control and Hospital Epidemiology*; 28:1275–1283.

members. Research also shows it feels even *better* if we believe we are looking out for those who are less able to access resources themselves ("less fortunate") and realistically, this is *why* it "feels good" to donate food/money/etc. to those who are in need.[7]

A recent study published in the *Journal of the American Medical Association* found that individuals who did *not* have a strong sense of their own purpose in daily life were *more than twice as likely to die* from health complications, especially those with cardiovascular issues.[8]

This strong association between a low level of purpose and higher risk of death for the participants of this study remained true regardless of how rich or poor they were and separate from any indicators of gender, race, or education level. In fact, researchers found this association to be *so* powerful that a life of purpose appeared to be more important for decreasing risk of death than more obviously unhealthy behaviors like *drinking, smoking,* or a *sedentary lifestyle* without regular exercise. These positive outcomes were largely linked to a *decrease in blood pressure* and *hormonal changes* that come with the body entering the *parasympathetic resting state*—allowing the natural systems of the mind and body to access their potential for self-healing and recovery.

Modern medicine has a lot of *chemicals* and *action points* to suggest and *prescribe*, but it is most important that people are able to function in their daily lives according to the design of our

---

7   Aknin, L. B., Dunn, E. W., and Norton, M. I. (2012). Happiness runs in a circular motion: Evidence for a positive feedback loop between prosocial spending and happiness. *Journal of Happiness Studies, 13,* 347–355. doi:10.1007/s10902-011-9267-5

8   Alimujiang, A., Wiensch, A., Boss, J. (2019). Association Between Life Purpose and Mortality Among US Adults Older Than 50 Years. *Journal of American Medicine Association*; 2(5):e194270. doi:10.1001/jamanetworkopen.2019.4270

DNA—to invest personal meaning into a daily life that satisfies a sense of life's purpose *with* and/or *for* others with whom we share our community.

The tricky part in modern society is to achieve a personal sense of life satisfaction that can be shared with other people *within* the experiences *themselves* in a way that creates meaningful connection between community members. This basic need could be met in the more traditional gender roles of provider and protector for most men up until recent history. But the corporate missions that have largely taken the place of human values no longer provide adequate connection between community members to meet this basic human need.

As the famous line from the movie *Fight Club* goes— "You're not your job. You're not how much money you have in the bank. You're not the car you drive. You're not the contents of your wallet. You're not your fucking khakis."[9] Many people are realizing this today in one way or another. No matter how much material resources a person consumes, this will not create a personal sense of happiness, nor will it create meaningful connection with others for a species that depends on social cohesion for quality of life and personal health.

This is where a concept of "purpose" comes into play for this book. Every person has their *own* unique reason for being alive, their *own* unique gifts to offer their community, and as a result, everyone is a bit *different*—having their own *interests*, *value systems* and *talents/resources* that should all play their own role in collaborative and dynamic group problem-solving. The more people think about themselves as social beings whose job it is to align with a sense of *purpose* as the source of intentional

---

9   Fincher, D., Linson, A., Chaffin, C., Bell, R. G., Uhls, J., Pitt, B., Norton, E.,... Twentieth Century Fox Home Entertainment, Inc. (2000). *Fight Club*. Beverly Hills, Calif: Twentieth Century Fox Home Entertainment.

decision-making in meaningful relationships, the easier it becomes to remain focused in serving our community with everything we have to offer in a way that also does no harm, as modeled by both Buddha and Jesus Christ alike. This is not only an ideal position for leadership, but also meets the health and well-being needs of mind and body—free from the pitfalls of "lifestyle creep" that turn people into obsessive "consumers" to fuel sales, rather than supporting functional community and healthy human beings.

CHAPTER 2: THE ORIGINS OF MAN—A HISTORICAL OVERVIEW

The world is going through a massive transition, and we can all feel it. In the last few hundred years, global population has increased from 1 billion to 7.7 billion.[10] As technology continues to develop, this dramatic change in population density—combined with rapid technological advancement—has created a new level of connection between all human beings on the planet that our species has never seen before.

This is placing an unprecedented amount of pressure on humankind to evolve as we face new demands characteristic of a global community, where we are not only biologically connected in the form of pathogens as seen in the recent Covid-19 pandemic, but also socially and culturally connected. The most recent developments of information technology and most notably, the proliferation of internet access has connected people across the globe to enable information sharing at a speed unlike ever before in human history. This ability to rapidly communicate ideas across the globe is a very helpful tool for sharing important information, but these new levels of increased connection have also forced different belief systems from previously isolated cultures to collide with more force than ever before—where it easily creates more tension and hostility between these groups in many cases.

For hundreds of thousands of years, human beings evolved as advanced primates who lived in highly social and interdependent communities. As our human ancestors left the

10   Max Roser, Hannah Ritchie and Esteban Ortiz-Ospina (2013) - "World Population Growth." *Published online at OurWorldInData.org.* Retrieved from: 'https://ourworldindata.org/world-population-growth' [Online Resource]

forests and began to hunt in the grasslands as a dynamic group, they were much more successful in hunting efforts than less socially evolved primates, who were not able to utilize elaborate group problem solving typical of our early ancestors.[11]

If matched in one-on-one direct competition with our closest living ancestor, the chimpanzee, a human would be outmatched every time because our physical body is *far* less powerful (we have roughly half of the "fast twitch muscle" as chimps), our canine teeth are pitifully smoothed down, and we have brittle fingernails where other animals have powerful claws.[12]

As our human ancestors became more successful with dynamic group hunting and tool use, the evolution of the human brain continued, rapidly outpacing other primates due to more exposure to nutrient-dense protein in a diet relatively high in meat as a result of successful hunting. For example, a chimpanzee's brain weighs 384 grams and requires roughly 2% of all nutrients available to their body, while an average human brain weighs 1,352 grams and requires roughly 20% of all nutrients available to our body![13]

---

11   Boyd, R., and Richerson, P. J. (2009). Culture and the evolution of human cooperation. *Philosophical transactions of the Royal Society of London. Series B, Biological sciences*, 364(1533), 3281–3288. https://doi.org/10.1098/rstb.2009.0134

12   Edwards, W. E., Clarke, T.E. (1965). Study of monkey, ape, and human morphology and physiology relating to strength and endurance, phase IX: The strength testing of five chimpanzee and seven human subjects. (Holloman Air Force Base, New Mexico 6571st Aeromedical Research Laboratory, Holloman, NM)

13   Mora-Bermúdez F, Badsha F, Kanton S, Camp JG, Vernot B, Köhler K, Voigt B, Okita K, Maricic T, He Z, Lachmann R, Pääbo S, Treutlein B, Huttner WB. Differences and similarities between human and chimpanzee neural progenitors during cerebral cortex development. eLife. 2016;5:e18683. doi: 10.7554/eLife.18683 - https://www.ncbi.nlm.nih.gov/pmc/articles/PMC7870144/

The success of our species has been defined by the ability to effectively live and work together in communities and this has consistently required dynamic group cooperation between community members. In direct response to these demands from of our environment, many important circuits of the human brain developed to rely on safe and secure social relationships with other community members to sustain optimal health and performance—both in body and mind.

Previous experiences with community members (especially family) will determine a person's future expectations regarding the assumed intentions by others with whom daily life is shared. This process of actively learning expectations for social relationships through personal experiences happens most rapidly in childhood with primary caretakers and takes place automatically, whether a person is consciously aware of it or not.

This has been clearly shown in the extensive research that began with the discovery of "social imprinting" in the 1950s,[14] then followed up by "attachment theory" in the 1970s.[15] It has since continued more dynamic development with later research from the pioneers of family psychotherapy,[16,17] as well as the foundation for the most heavily supported evidence-based model of modern couples therapy in "emotion focused

---

14   Bowlby, J. (1988). *A secure base: Parent-child attachment and healthy human development*. Basic Books.
15   Ainsworth, M. D. S., Blehar, M. C., Waters, E., and Wall, S. (1978). *Patterns of attachment: A psychological study of the strange situation*. Lawrence Erlbaum.
16   Satir, V. (1988). *The new peoplemaking*. Science and Behavior Books.
17   Bowen, M. (1978). *Family therapy in clinical practice*. New York: Jason Aronson.

therapy."[18] In fact, some of the most valuable information from this bed of research will provide the foundation for the skills taught later in this book.

The evolutionary relationship between our changing environments, the community-oriented nature of our basic needs, and the development of the human brain has taken place over six million years since our earliest ancestors. As a result of this long process, there are some aspects of our being, or humanity, if you will, that every person shares as a member of a highly social species.

The dynamic cooperation and problem solving between community members that facilitated our success as a species also supported the development of verbal speech as we know spoken language today. This required the development of required organs—our esophagus, larynx, tongue, and lips—to work together in ways that are capable of creating a wide diversity of sounds rarely found in any other species of the animal kingdom.

A significant survival benefit of spoken language is the ability to pass down oral tradition from one generation to the next. This invaluable information contained inside stories traditionally told at fireside along drums and dance held the keys to ongoing survival for each community of individuals in their own unique environment.

The relative power of verbal communication and its ability to encode vital information for community survival is shown in the anatomy of human beings. We have developed a *larynx* (also called our "voice box") capable of creating a wide range of sounds with our mouth, throat, and tongue, alongside our

---

18   Johnson, S. M. (2009). Attachment theory and emotionally focused therapy for individuals and couples: Perfect partners. In J. H. Obegi and E. Berant (Eds.), Attachment theory and research in clinical work with adults (p. 410–433). The Guilford Press.

relatively large human brain. The combination gave us the ability to not only communicate a wide range of sounds and words, but also to create abstract concepts for dynamic problem solving and cooperation. Further, we could then encode this knowledge for future generations in the form of oral traditions that keep a community together through shared cultures and social expectations.[19] Altogether, these abilities represented an evolutionary advantage for humans that allowed us to create greater safety and security from a community-based lifestyle.

The vital information encoded within spoken language included two aspects of ongoing survival of each community.[20] First, there is literal information about how to carry out essential activities for survival of daily life, like securing food sources and medicinal practices.

The second area is more abstract, but in many ways just as essential: to pass along mythos containing important allegories and life lessons that functioned as an organizing force for each unique culture. These stories are complete with specific belief systems and behavior expectations that maintain the meaning, functionality, and order required for each community to ensure ongoing survival against the relative chaos of the natural world.

A clear example of the first aspect of language can be found in the use of the "sago plant" as the main carbohydrate source in the diet of many communities found in Southeast Asia and New Guinea.[21] Believe it or not, the sago plant is highly poisonous

19   Belin P. (2006). Voice processing in human and non-human primates. *Philosophical transactions of the Royal Society of London. Series B, Biological sciences, 361*(1476), 2091–2107. https://doi.org/10.1098/rstb.2006.1933

20   Minc, L.D. (1986). *Scarcity and survival: the role of oral tradition in mediating subsistence crises.* Journal of Anthropological Archeology 5: 39-113.

21   Lal, J. J. (2003). "SAGO PALM." *Encyclopedia of Food Sciences and Nutrition.* pp. 5035–5039. doi:10.1016/B0-12-227055-X/01036-1. ISBN 9780122270550.

in its raw form, but by using a process passed through the generations over thousands of years, it can be prepared with hand tools for safe consumption. And don't be fooled—the use of hand tools does not make it an easy task! Rather, a dynamic, complicated multi-day process is required for safe consumption. This important skill set would likely have been *impossible* to rediscover by every subsequent generation without clear instruction passed down from community elders.

An example of the second more abstract aspect of language can be found in the ten commandments of the Old Testament (or "Torah" in Judaism), that became the basis for Judeo-Christian religions. This collection of guidelines can be seen as a helpful outline to direct community life in general. If we look at these ten commandments as more general community guidelines to prevent dishonesty, infidelity, stealing, and to protect the wisdom of the elders, then it is easy to see how these are all important expectations in their own right if community members are to exist harmoniously and sustainably.

There are roughly 6,500 different languages spoken in the world today[22] and even though there is a wide range of diversity in the languages themselves, the importance of verbal speech when it comes to human life—whether male or female—cannot be understated.

With this said, there *have* been some very important differences between the traditional roles of men versus women, based on functions of survival and resulting behavior expectations to execute these functions. These behavioral expectations are grouped into "roles" that reflect a socially-recognized pattern that is reinforced through cultural

---

22   Romaine, Suzanne. 2000. *Language in Society.* 2nd ed. Oxford: Oxford University Press

expectations that, in turn, is meant to support the success of each community from one generation to the next.

The "gender role" for women has historically been a primary focus on the essential role of childbirth, as well as their physical body being the only food source for human newborns through the first several months of life. As a result, it was *not* an option to place females in higher risk situations because their death meant the end of childbearing for that family—an essential requirement of natural selection. Since the community could not put the physical safety of women at risk if it were to survive into the next generation, it became the role of men to be the primary hunter and warrior, now called "provider and protector," for women, children, and elders in order to ensure survival of the community.

Males grew physically wider shoulders for throwing objects with greater power and precision to facilitate efficient hunting and war tactics. In order to support childbirth in a species with a relatively enormous brain, women grew wider hips to accommodate passage of a large head through the birth canal.

Around 300,000 years ago in what is called the "Paleolithic Era," our ancestors physically, mentally, and socially evolved into the human beings we are today, while living in hunter-gatherer societies that followed a preferred food source from season to season.[23] Anthropologists and archaeologists have found clear evidence from around 12,000 years ago, after the last great ice age, that human societies began to move towards farming communities in what is commonly called the age of agriculture, or "Neolithic Revolution." Up to that point, human communities gathered nutrients from whatever plants were

23   University of Zurich. (2020, February 28). Hunter-gatherer networks accelerated human evolution. *ScienceDaily*. Retrieved February 20, 2021 from www.sciencedaily.com/releases/2020/02/200228142013.htm

available as they grew naturally in their original ecosystems, a practice called "horticulture," as opposed to "agriculture," which is characterized by the growth of plants in permanent settlements in a man-made food chain along with the raising of animals.

These farming communities of the Neolithic Revolution reflected the first permanent communities of human beings since our origins as hunter-gatherers. These more stable and consistent farming communities came with significant advantages for ongoing survival, including the reliability of food production. That reliability in turn brought about the first significant food surpluses. To manage the food surpluses and additional population it could now support, communities created various organizational structures that promoted the development of more stable infrastructure to maintain this higher level of food production.[24] Even though there were many adaptive functions for survival, it is also important to mention that farming narrowed down the food sources available, which in turn has led to a downturn in the quality of human nutrition.[25]

These early communities were also largely isolated from one another as a means for each community to protect itself from "outsiders," who were viewed as a threat to their survival. Each community developed its own cultural expectations that became more rigid to meet the growing demands of consistency required by farming communities. A shared culture helped to not only create cohesion through mutual meaning-making, but also prescribed social expectations for thoughts, feelings,

24   Weiss, E., and Zohary, D. (2011). The Neolithic Southwest Asian Founder Crops: Their Biology and Archaeobotany. *Current Anthropology,* *52*(S4), S237-S254. doi:10.1086/658367
25   Armelagos, George J. (2014). "Brain Evolution, The Determinants Of Food Choice, And The Omnivore's Dilemma." *Critical Reviews in Food Science and Nutrition.* 54 (10): 1330–1341. DOI:10.1080/10408398.2011.6358 17. ISSN 1040-8398. PMID 24564590.

behavior, and belief systems. Those social expectations served to maintain the required level of reliability and structure for daily life in a community where this was essential for survival.

It is important to mention that while mating pairs between men and women have always been commonplace, the practice of courtship, dating, and romance was *not* commonly practiced until very recently in human history. In fact, romance was for the most part believed to only bring instability as a result of lust and passion, both of which being associated at the time with sex workers and young people "on the prowl" whose behavior was largely responsible for unplanned pregnancy out of wedlock. This behavior was viewed as a threat to the very foundation of safety and security that farming communities relied upon for ongoing survival. Instead, politically-arranged marriages were intentionally made between family gatekeepers to protect the lineage of property ownership for future generations.

As an interesting sidenote, the famous Greek philosopher Plato spoke about the importance of a union between sexual partners that is based on shared meaning and values, rather than lust—which is not reliable and can be expected to fade over time. [26] This is why a relationship focused on friendship is called "platonic." It turns out a strong friendship at the foundation of committed romantic relationships is directly related to not only relationship success, but also personal health and well-being. Maybe the elders were right when they advised to "focus on friendship first."

Perhaps unsurprisingly, the first records of organized religion also began to pop up around the same time period that isolated farming communities became so successful. While

---

26   Messman, S. J., Hause, D. J., and Hause, K. S. (2000). "Motives to Remain Platonic, Equity, and the Use of Maintenance Strategies in Opposite-Sex Friendships." *Journal of Social and Personal Relationships*, **17** (1), 67–94. doi:10.1177/0265407500171004

archaeologists and cultural anthropologists have found clear evidence in gravesites that human communities practiced forms of spirituality starting at least 300,000 years ago,[27] the first *written* records of highly-structured religious practices that we commonly understand as "organized religion" today began with the isolated farming communities of the Neolithic Era.

Religious practices provided a valuable tool for further reinforcing the culture of each community, providing maintenance for social expectations and behavior that promoted consistency and structure. In addition to the specific instructions for chaotic and uncertain times, religions also established more general guidance for other social behavior by defining the "normal behavior" found in each society, including knowledge, belief systems, arts, law, customs, and the abilities of the individuals found in each group. These shared ways of understanding the world through religion provided another layer of stability for a shared community mission based on a set of values.

With religion came two clear benefits for ongoing survival. First, these practices created order from the relative chaos early humans perceived from the natural world, before an understanding of science could offer an explanation for the events in daily life. Second, this highly integrated and shared way of understanding the world also provided a powerful level of influence on the behavior of community members, as seen fit by the leader(s) of each isolated farming community. Not surprisingly, different organized religions sprang up all around the world due both to their highly-adaptive organizing functions in community settings and the power they bestowed upon their leaders.

---

27   Andre Leroi-Gourhan and Annette Michelson, "The Religion of the Caves: Magic or Metaphysics?" *The MIT Press*, Vol, 37, October 1986, pp. 6-17

Due to the different roles historically available to men and women, the cultural expectations for each gender have been created to support these divergent roles. Oftentimes, religious doctrine was used to reinforce these expectations of "normalcy." Starting out as fierce hunters and warriors in the origins of our ancestors, the social and cultural expectations for men and boys have actually not moved too far away from these rough and rugged beginnings. In many ways, the gender expectations for men have largely continued from the original roots as a hunter/ warrior but have just been renamed "provider/protector" over the years.

These gender roles will be referred to as those of "traditional manhood" and still live on today as the dominant cultural standards that shape social and personal life. These belief systems and behavioral expectations of *traditional manhood* made for fierce hunters and warriors in the Old World. However, the current context of human social development requires an update of these qualities to remain socially and personally adaptive, and ultimately for men to remain healthy in modern society. We will briefly outline these traits of *traditional manhood* below for reference before a more thorough description later in this book:

1. Success based on achievement in competition against and comparison to others.

2. Emotional Restriction ("stoicism") where anger is always acceptable and happiness is tolerated in *small* doses, but not too much or it is seen as a sign of "femininity."

3. Strength and Courage as shown by a willingness to engage in duties eagerly and willingly, while never showing pain or fear, at risk of looking "weak and insecure."

4. Independence as shown by a willingness to engage in duties on individual merit and ability—never asking for help, at the risk of looking "unreliable" or "stupid."

5. Acceptance of Coercion (use of personal power— even violence) to control an outcome as accepted methods to "get the job done."

6. Avoidance of "Female Qualities" that are rarely defined explicitly, but more understood as the polar opposite of the "traditional manhood qualities" outlined above—including low influence, emotional expression, lacking strength, dependence, and submission.

There are still important places for these traits, but when they are relied upon too heavily or used in conjunction with each other, they easily result in "gender role strain" for men. *Gender role strain* can be defined as "rigid, sexist, or restrictive gender roles, learned during socialization, that result in personal restriction, devaluation, or violation of others and self."[28] Altogether, research has shown that men experience gender role strain in meeting social, emotional, and even basic safety needs.[29] Gender role strain will be addressed in greater detail in chapter 4, alongside evidence-based suggestions and solutions for resolving these issues.

So as we've seen, the Neolithic Revolution brought farming communities and their cultural expectations across the world— complete with more established gender roles (specifically

28   O'Neil, J. M. (1990). Assessing men's gender role conflict. In D. Moore, and F. Leafgren (Eds.), *Problem solving strategies and interventions for men in conflict* (pp. 23–38). Alexandria, VA: American Counseling Association.
29   O'Neil, J. M. (2015). *Men's gender role conflict: Psychological costs, consequences, and an agenda for change.* Washington, DC: American Psychological Association.

in terms of male control of resources through physical dominance),[30] traditional romantic relationship expectations, and the proliferation of organized religion. These were the standard social, and cultural expectations that remained largely unchanged in human civilizations for roughly 10,000 years until the relatively recent "Industrial Revolution" began in the mid-1700s.

The *Industrial Revolution* brought urban development and with this, came the associated economic, social and community developments associated with "city life." It is important to note that these urban developments did not reach all corners of the world at the same time. For metropolitan areas along central waterways used for international trade—like Paris, London, New York, and Amsterdam—these urban changes began much earlier than in more historically rural areas—like most of North America, Australia, Russia, and the Middle East.

As a result, different areas of the world, or even different regions within a single country, can be in drastically different points of transition regarding these traditional cultural expectations. As a result, it is common to see different levels of readiness and willingness to change those same models. This has often taken the form of sociopolitical tension between communities that historically lived in isolated rural areas versus those who have been exposed to greater cultural variation in more diverse metropolitan areas.

Not only did the Industrial Revolution facilitate cultural mixing between previously isolated communities, but it also came with significant developments in the workplace and economy. It introduced machines that replaced production by hand and

---

30   Cintas-Peña, M., and García Sanjuán, L. (2019). Gender Inequalities in Neolithic Iberia: A Multi-Proxy Approach. *European Journal of Archaeology,* *22*(4), 499-522. doi:10.1017/eaa.2019.3

factories with systematized assembly lines of these machines that enabled mass production. Laborers were also needed to operate the machines in the newly-built factories, so urban areas were constructed to house the first industrial workers.[31] People subsequently poured into cities from the surrounding farming communities, whether to escape religious persecution, war, or famine or just in search of new opportunities. This represented the first large shift away from people living in the isolated farming communities of the Old World into the more culturally interconnected landscape of Modern Society.

People from these isolated communities often chose the same geographic region to live and work together in urban areas. By settling in the same neighborhoods, these groups were able to hold on to some of the traditions and cultural expectations of their original communities. This is one reason that it was so popular for specific cultural groups to live in distinct locations within these urban areas for personal safety and security—like the "ChinaTown" and "Little Italy" found in New York City.

However, those communities could no longer strictly adhere to all of their traditions, nor could they expect those around them to comply with their "in-group" expectations. Rather, each person and each community had to become much more flexible regarding the new people they encountered, who were now more than likely coming from other cultures and communities. This has proven to be a difficult task for a species who has always relied on the cultural expectations of our original tribe as the "normal model" for daily life over hundreds of thousands of years.

---

31   Horn, Jeff; Rosenband, Leonard; Smith, Merritt (2010). *Reconceptualizing the Industrial Revolution*. Cambridge MA, London: MIT Press. ISBN 978-0-262-51562-7.

The new urban marketplaces ushered in by the Industrial Revolution created new economic opportunity and options for providing financial resources, but the newfound advantages of corporations also chiseled away at the market share that was previously secured by family-owned businesses. In 1830, 70% of the free market was owned by family-owned businesses. By 1870 this number decreased to only 30% ,where it has remained largely unchanged over the last 150 years.

These statistics paint a picture of huge economic changes with corporate interests being able to outpace family-owned businesses at a dramatic rate. In only forty years, from 1830-1870, most family-owned companies went out of business. To this day, corporate interests continue to drive the economic output of modern society in an even more fast-paced global community, where efficiency and cost-cutting are made possible by mass production that family-owned businesses struggle to compete with.

In 1865, 60% of Americans still worked and lived on their family farm of origin. By the early 1900s, most of the economy and workforce transitioned to factory production in densely-populated urban areas, where they remain today. This means that even today, most people are only a few generations away from rural farming communities. With this historical context in mind, it is probably not a surprise to see that the cultural expectations of the Old World continue to live on largely untouched today in many American families and communities. In the grand scheme of human cultural history this is an incredibly recent transition.

This transition from the isolated farming communities of the Old World into a more urban, culturally-diverse, and population-dense setting was a dramatic shift in how human beings functioned in our day-to-day lives. We have always been a social and community-driven species, but we have also been largely isolated within our given culture of origin. Our evolution as human beings has created a very tribal species who affiliates strongly with an "in-group," while remaining prone to seeing those with different cultural practices as "outsiders." The perspective of *insider* versus *outsider* is largely defined by different cultural practices that are neutral in their own right but have always represented a threat in the form of competition for resources and livelihood. Now all of our different tribes have been forcefully poured into the same social ecosystem with the emergence of a global community. At first this occurred physically with the urbanization of the Industrial Revolution. Then more recently, technological connectivity has merged our social lives. And now, with the recent pandemic, we see how our physical connectivity also means that we are biologically connected.

While this is certainly a fascinating period for anthropologists, sociologists, and epidemiologists alike, this shift has also caused major disruptions to human life in almost every way.

CHAPTER 3: PREPARING FOR A HEALING JOURNEY

Humankind has come a long way since our humble beginnings but in most cases, people still tend to be raised and therefore primarily socialized, by our immediate family. It is almost impossible to grow up without *at least some* influence from the belief systems and behavioral expectations of the Old World—traditional gender roles included. In general, these roles include some variation of men as provider/protector and women as nurturer/homemaker.

My intention is not to imply that traditional gender roles only offer one way for a person to act. First, each culture or tradition that a person identifies with may offer a different way to approach a given situation that is acceptable within their culture. There is also a great deal of variety amongst people in how they embody that traditional definition (or not), which creates each individual's unique self-identity. Those different aspects of personal identity also interact and overlap with other cultural expectations about gender, race, sex, age, etc. Those overlaps are referred to as "intersections" in the field of social sciences.[32] Each *intersection* comes with its own specific set of cultural expectations and social pressures in each unique context of life functioning. These combinations create a *lot* of cultural variation for people on an individual level across different contexts of day-to-day life, despite the similar foundation of traditional gender roles from the Old World that we all share to some degree.

---

32   American Psychological Association. (2017). *Multicultural guidelines: An ecological approach to context, identity, and intersectionality.* https://www.apa.org/about/policy/multicultural-guidelines

While many people assume "men and boys are all the same," along the lines of traditional gender roles, this is incredibly short-sighted and surface-level thinking. In fact, men and boys are a very diverse group of human beings with *many different* intersecting identities themselves that make us all unique in our own ways.

In order to explain this concept of a single person having multiple identities, I will use myself as an example. I am a man who is, at this point in history, generally recognized in social spaces as "white."

I am also Jewish by cultural affiliation and bloodline alike. I came of age as an active member of my religious congregation (called a "synagogue"), where I learned to identify with Judaism and other Jewish people.

I also identify intimately with my own unique healing journey and with it, what has become my life's work as a healer and protector of vulnerable community members through servant leadership.

I certainly have more than just these three aspects to my identity, but these three sources are sufficient to illustrate the *intersections* that create variation in social expectations.

I am generally seen as "white" as long as I am not being "too Jewish," like when I am walking out of synagogue or openly speaking about Jewish culture. In those cases I am more likely to be perceived as "non-white" by certain cultures or individuals and as a result, am often given less access to "in-group social status" in those cases.

In my work as a healer of wounded and/or vulnerable community members, my physical appearance as a white man with a shaved head has at times been perceived to resemble an "aggressive look" that has no place in healing spaces and no place within their community.

I can recall times in my own life when developing my own self-identity *relied* on my ability to separate some aspects of traditional manhood expectations from my own authentic self-identity. The deeply personal task of exposing unconscious belief systems and old engrained habits as no longer helpful— even harmful to health and happiness—is *much* easier said than done. The complication arises because the influence from traditional manhood can be convenient and effective for gaining control of a given situation in the short-term. But those same behaviors can become barriers to psychological and personal development themselves, because they reinforce a person's "comfort zone" for the good, bad and ugly. This feedback loop tends to remain stuck until someone is all but *forced* outside of their familiar world to meet new demands associated with life's changing circumstances.

Before we take a closer look at the impacts of traditional manhood on society, it is important to note that all people— men included—have a very difficult relationship with change, especially as this relates to personal worldview. Human beings have been not only surviving but thriving as a species due to our social nature, which has placed even more demands on these social tools because they have been so adaptive through history.

It was noted earlier that the human brain increased in size by roughly four times from our closest relative the chimpanzee. Those physical changes to our brain took place largely to accommodate the dynamic social relationships that characterize human life. There are two main components required for these dynamic social relationships—one is an awareness of "self" and the second is an awareness of "other." Both are required to have a stable self-identity for group belonging.

All human beings—regardless of gender or sex—tend to understand themselves as more separate from other people and our natural ecosystem than we actually are in reality. The term "egocentric" is used to describe a worldview based on the false assumption that everyone else should have the same personal opinions that we do. This is certainly short-sighted, but it is also a perfectly natural tendency for all human beings, who experience the world very symbolically.

Symbolic experience means that we as humans do not experience the world exactly as it is. Instead, we create symbols, words, and categories. We then create concepts and beliefs about those various symbols, categories and words. For example, when you see the word "dog," it is merely a collection of marks on a piece of paper, but it conjures the concept of a four-legged canine. For you, it might bring up the image of a very specific creature, perhaps your personal pet. It may also make you remember an experience with a dog, for good or for bad. All of that arises for us out of mere squiggles and it is different for every single person. The more *egocentric* an individual is, the more they tend to believe that everyone has the same personal experience that they do.

Symbolic experience has always come in handy for survival because it allows human beings to categorize other people and/or experiences as threats versus non-threats quickly and subconsciously, without much personal energy spent on this very important task. We do not have to constantly consciously assess everything we see for danger. Having an egocentric worldview simplifies things further by assuming that everyone else also perceives things as you do. To put it plainly, symbolic experience in our worldview allows our *ego* to have a sense of control in everyday life and prevents us from having a *complete mental breakdown* regarding the very real chaos of the natural world.

In many ways, this naturally occurring egocentric worldview serves as reinforcement for a personal sense of order and control in everyday life by decreasing anxiety regarding fear of the unknown. That in turn allows increased focus on the immediate tasks at hand for problem solving. While being *egocentric* has been a helpful shortcut for surviving daily life through the evolution of our ancestors, this now cuts many people off from thriving, or sometimes even surviving, in modern society.

For example, most people would agree that losing a loved one is a difficult and painful experience. In fact, anyone who tries to dispute the pain associated with personal loss is either consciously lying or is missing some essential centers of brain function associated with "empathy" that is characteristic of "Antisocial Personality Disorder" (used to be called "sociopath"—the personality typology of serial killers). The name for this process of personal loss is technically called "grief," but people rarely consider the fact that we often go through a similar process when there is a loss of *personal identity*. Human beings are social animals and our connections to other people tend to be guarded tightly. Psychologists have found that our relationship to our own worldview is often protected *even more forcefully*!

When people try to shift their worldview too quickly, there tends to be a lot of resistance to the new ideas. Whether consciously or subconsciously, it puts a lot of what we perceive as order and structure at a relatively high-risk of *chaos*. This resistance is only natural and the associated anxiety should not be perceived as a sign of personal "weakness." However, it can become problematic if we allow the anxiety to convince us that we should remain inside of our comfort zone, clutching on to old ways as the environment continues to change.

In addition to a sense of loss in personal worldview, growing past old limiting beliefs also involves a more thorough and critical analysis of our own family culture where we originated. It is common to experience a degree of guilt because this critical analysis can feel like an act of "disloyalty" to our origins. This sense of loyalty to where we came should be seen as a *strength* and not a weakness. But once we recognize our worldview is harming ourselves or others, it is our responsibility to do better by ourselves, our loved ones and the community members that rely on us as sources of justice and empowerment.

This process of releasing old worldviews and belief systems has been found to be accompanied by some of the same experiences associated with *grief*. While these experiences are normal, they are also a sign that the mind and body is "having a reaction" that is uncomfortable and must be honored. But it is *not* a sign that the exposure is unhealthy or unhelpful! Instead, think of it like the soreness from a hard workout the day before. You cannot expect to grow and be stronger—physically, mentally, or spiritually—without some discomfort and pain. It is simply part of the growth process.

The following stages of grief have been studied at length through the history of psychology[33] and while there could be a whole separate book on this experience of letting go, we will only briefly explain this process so you can monitor your own reactions and remain in control of your own healing process.

---

33   Kübler-Ross, E., and Kessler, D. (2005). *On grief and grieving: Finding the meaning of grief through the five stages of loss.* New York: Scribner

1. Denial/Shock—Denial helps us survive the initial jolt of loss. In this stage, the world would lack meaning without that part of reality that we once depended on. It is easy to become overwhelmed by this lack of meaning, so it is common to respond with avoidance—the cornerstone of *denial/shock*. While *denial* might not seem helpful at first glance, it helps us cope with the abrupt change/loss by pacing our feelings, rather than getting overwhelmed with attempting integration of the big picture all at one time. As a person begins to start asking questions about the possible presence of the loss, this is a sign they are beginning to accept the changed reality. This is a sign of gaining personal strength and awareness as the denial fades, but the following stages are more consciously uncomfortable as all of the previously repressed feelings come to the surface.

2. Anger—Anger is a necessary stage because it *wakes us up* to the loss and provides personal motivation to process it. The anger also protects the more vulnerable emotions underneath of it until the time is right to work through them more directly. It is OK to feel angry because the more you allow yourself to feel it, the more it can be processed so the user can make room for recovering and adapting to the change. There are other emotions under the anger, but for now the anger tends to feel safe and protective, so be patient with this innate protective wisdom of the psyche. It is common to direct the anger towards others—friends, family, healthcare providers—even God. The anger can be a welcomed source of energy to attempt interaction with someone rather than getting lost in a state of overwhelm about the recent loss. It's important to remember that the anger is just another indication of the intensity of our love, loyalty, and respect for the loss.

3. Bargaining—When we perceive a possible loss in the near future, people tend to start bargaining with themselves—even God—for a sense of influence or control over the loss so that it might be avoided. It is common for people to get lost in a personal maze of "If only…" or "What if…" statements that are designed to convince ourselves that we could have helped avoid the loss. Guilt is often very present at this stage as we find fault in ourselves for not being diligent about what we "think" we could have done differently.

4. Integration/Depression—After bargaining, we can direct our attention to the loss itself. Empty feelings of sadness come forward to take away our energy and motivation for daily life—almost like a temporary depression. Even though the sadness often feels like it will last forever, it is important to lean in and let it unfold. This is the appropriate response to an important loss, but it is common for people to see this as a state we need to "snap out of," especially for men, due to a temporary lack of motivation that decreases immediate ability to labor for economic productivity, which tends to almost feel like a personal offense to men that have been raised to believe personal achievement is essential for success and happiness. Even though sadness is not usually within a man's emotional comfort zone, it must occur to some degree in order to honor this natural human experience so that we can move forward with the appropriate adaptations. An inability to do so will result in spending one's life bracing for an impact that has already occurred or living in regret about something in the past that cannot be changed.

5. Resolution/Acceptance—This stage is about accepting the changed reality in the present—that we lost something or someone very important to us. This does not make the loss "OK" in that it feels indifferent, but the loss can be accepted as a fact of our past life experiences. We learn how to actively adjust our worldview and our daily existence, rather than trying to leave everything as it was in the past—before the loss. We must learn to reorganize our roles, catch the old thoughts and feelings, interrupt the old habits, and establish new routines for coping with daily stressors—sometimes even readjusting entire belief systems to make room for more significant adaptations. It is common for the guilt to re-emerge here, as we begin to live our lives in the present with the needed adjustments and as a result, begin to feel better—like we are betraying ourselves or someone we loved. This is natural, but we are the only person who gets to control our daily choices. Instead of pushing our feelings down, we must learn to listen to the underlying needs beneath them.

It is also important to mention that while these stages are normal and to be expected as part of an experience of personal loss, the process of grieving itself is *dynamic*. We do not go into each individual stage, work through it to full resolution, and then move on to the next stage in a linear fashion. It is common to feel one, then another, and back again to the first one until the process of healing from the loss and integrating new life lessons is complete. As we explore the ideas in this book—some of which might be new and personally challenging—I encourage you to keep this framework of grief in mind to better understand your own experiences with "letting go."

Now, let's shed some light on the global state of men's health in modern society. It is actually much more at risk than you might have realized! For what it is worth, it is my hope that the reader does not allow a personal sense of failure or insecurity about this naively blissful lack of personal awareness to linger too long. Even mental health providers who have studied this area professionally have a hard time adequately serving men with mental health symptoms, because men do *not* tend to behave in the ways that psychologists, counselors, and therapists are trained to assess and intervene.[34] If mental health professionals have such a hard time seeing the difference between a man's true personality and his mental health issues, then how does it make sense for a man to put this pressure on *himself* until we know better?

Since the expectations for traditional manhood are so woven into the social and cultural norms of society-at-large, this tends to be an area of life where many men stay in denial about the unhealthy use of our social influence. It is difficult because these behaviors and belief systems are so insulated on a personal, relational, as well as institutional level. In addition, since the very nature of a "social privilege" refers to personal advantages secured by those who have access, it is common that people don't want to let it go. I mean...who would get to the Super Bowl, win the coin toss, then punt the ball to the *other* team?

---

34   Cochran, S. V. & Rabinowitz, F. E. (2000). *Men and depression: Clinical and empirical perspectives.* San Diego, CA: Academic Press.

This is particularly true if those advantages feel as though they are part of a system that has a set, or "finite," number of resources available. If we believe that we are in a situation where one group, say women, gaining more access to resources means that the other group, say men, must lose those resources, then men expect to experience a personal loss, *even where no personal loss will actually occur.* Research shows there is considerable evidence that *most* men share this false belief—also known as "scarcity bias."[35]

These traditional gender roles are still relevant for male identity in modern society to a certain degree—after all, men are still not capable of childbirth and there will always be at least some threat of harm to vulnerable community members where the strongest bodies will be needed to protect and serve. With this said, a strict or rigid adherence to the social and behavioral codes found in traditional gender roles are oftentimes not conducive to human beings living authentic, happy, and healthy lives in modern society for both men and women alike. In fact, a more rigid adherence in either direction often creates imbalance both interpersonally (with others) and intrapersonally (within ourselves).

---

35   Cassino, Dan. "Why More American Men Feel Discriminated Against." Harvard Business Review. September 29, 2016. https://hbr.org/2016/09/why-more-american-men-feel-discriminated-against

CHAPTER 4: IDENTITY CRISIS FUELING THE MEN'S HEALTH CRISIS

All human beings have a sense of personal identity that is used to navigate daily life. This sense of "self" is essential for all people because we are socially driven, and this consistent sense of identity gives us and those around us a standard set of expectations for interacting with us as part of a system of social relationships. While some parts of this identity often have some basis in our authentic interests and preferences, most of what people consider their "self-identity" is actually *ego*—a collection of habits (also called "defense mechanisms") that protect our comfort zones—based on meeting social and cultural expectations in our personal life up to this point in time.

A *defense mechanism* is a mental and emotional habit that distorts our personal reality in order to protect a relative comfort zone against feelings of anxiety and impulses that are understood as unacceptable to maintain personal identity and important social bonds.[36] These are internalized lessons from our previous life experiences that we subconsciously use to protect and preserve our *self-identity* as we know it. We also use them to ensure we are not deemed unworthy of acceptance by our tribe and rejected as a result—a "life sentence" for human beings over hundreds of thousands of years of our evolution.

It is important to remember that a *defense mechanism* is unconsciously created to reinforce a personal sense of stability in a chaotic world—rooted in both *self-identity* and *social*

36   Schacter, D. L., Gilbert, D. T., and Wegner, D. M. (2011). *Psychology.* New York, NY: Worth Publishers.

identity. The very function of a *defense mechanism* is to protect conscious awareness from very real fears of chaos and the unknown. This is why a *defense mechanism* is not experienced consciously because if it were, it would no longer serve their function of protecting the user as a distraction from a painful and/or threatening reality. The only way to increase conscious awareness of these defense mechanisms is by *forcing* oneself outside of your comfort zone.

This process of personal growth and development is very difficult for men because it demands an acceptance of not knowing "the right answer," a personal experience of emotional discomfort and even asking for help in a way that can feel dependent and weak. As a result, most men do not give themselves a chance to develop more conscious awareness of their defense mechanisms because this requires an acceptance of the personal shortcomings that often come as a *direct* result of relying on the leverage provided by *male privilege* as taught and then reinforced socially/culturally by traditional manhood.

As discussed in detail in the last chapter, since the beginning of our species, human beings have lived in groups of meaningfully-connected community members to support basic needs of survival. But humanity is beginning to reflect a more global community. Unless we can return to our genetic roots as a highly-evolved social species, our basic needs for wellness and life satisfaction *cannot* be adequately satisfied. These social and political changes might have unfolded more quickly than previous "social revolutions," but when it comes down to human beings as a species, the basic needs themselves have not changed much, if at *all*.

In fact, research still shows that when it comes to human needs for health and wellness across our lifespan, there is one variable that becomes more important than anything else.

Beyond access to adequate medical care, the most important factor for longevity and quality of life is having meaningful and satisfying social relationships[37,38]—still in line with the primary needs of our ancestors for millions of years.

In order to re-introduce and re-integrate the required belief systems and behaviors for meeting these basic human needs, most men must first experience their own process of "deconversion" from traditional manhood of the Old World to make room for this type of personal growth.

This is *not* an easy or comfortable process, but like getting stronger in the gym or losing weight by eating healthier food, the pay-off to our health and wellness is significant. This requires men to release these ingrained and often very personal ways of seeing ourselves and the world around us through the process of *grief* just described in the last chapter. It would be common to experience a range of emotions at different points moving forward, since there will be very clear descriptions of the belief systems that men typically use to reinforce these traditional worldviews. The human awaiting to emerge from within appreciates your patience with these potential reactions—even if it feels difficult at times—and trusts that you will find the fuel for your fire in the natural wisdom that comes out as a result of this growth process.

While this can be uncomfortable in the moment, it is an essential part of coming to terms with who we are *not* so that this precious life is not spent chasing someone else's dreams. Once we have increased awareness about the trappings of traditional

37   Umberson, D., and Montez, J. K. (2010). Social relationships and health: a flashpoint for health policy. *Journal of health and social behavior, 51 Suppl*(Suppl), S54–S66. https://doi.org/10.1177/0022146510383501

38   George E. Vaillant; Charles C. McArthur; and Arlie Bock, 2010, "Grant Study of Adult Development, 1938-2000," https://doi.org/10.7910/ DVN/48WRX9, Harvard Dataverse, V4

manhood associated with gaining social influence through *male privilege*, we can explore the solutions for tapping in to a more authentic *self-identity* that allows access to a full range of human experiences for accessing the potential strength, resilience, and healing in a meaningful daily life with our loved ones.

Let's take a look at the barriers commonly faced by men when it comes to pushing past these old limiting beliefs. Clarity around these barriers—what we will refer to as "Man Myths" below—must be identified and overcome by men in our own personal lives in order to access healing properties underneath.

1. Man Myth—Success comes from winning in competition against others

The more someone focuses on winning in competition as the primary goal, the more they develop "scarcity bias,"[39] a social phenomenon where people place higher value on resources in short supply and a lower value on whatever is perceived to be in abundance. This is a mental shortcut that places relative value on an item based on how easily it could be lost to competitors, with "being the winner" as the ideal focus of this scarcity mindset. This makes for fierce competitors in hunting and war, but it also leads to systemic errors in thinking—called "thinking errors" or "cognitive biases" in psychology and behavioral sciences—that disrupt the overall quality of rational judgment.[40]

In reality, life satisfaction comes from being connected in our social bonds *while* we persevere meaningfully as a community through trials and tribulations by adhering to

---

39   Mittone, L. and Savadori, L. (2009), The Scarcity Bias. *Applied Psychology, 58*: 453-468. https://doi.org/10.1111/j.1464-0597.2009.00401.x
40   Haselton, M.,G., Nettle, D., Andrews, P.,W., (2005). "The Evolution of the Cognitive Bias." In Buss DM (ed.). *The Handbook of Evolutionary Psychology*. Hoboken, NJ, US: John Wiley and Sons Inc. pp. 724–746.

shared personal values. By sharing these values as a part of collaborative problem solving, this creates shared meaning that reinforces the social bonds essential for holding a community together. If we learn to base our personal value on dominance against others in our last performance, this tends to be a set-up for failure in our personal relationships, who are inevitably on the other side of being dominated.

Even if it were possible to be the best in our environment at all times, who would we have to share the spoils of war if we have behaved so poorly on the field of battle that other people could not trust or feel understood by us? How could we then expect to be understood by them so we can actually enjoy *anything* in this life? An overfocus on winning in competition blocks men from meaningful relationships with others because it is all too easy for men to become more focused on winning than respecting the other people in the shared experience enough to maintain their trust in the long run.

Even in cases where the reader is thinking, "let the best man win," no matter how proficient we learn to be in the tasks that make up our community role(s), there can always be a bigger and faster dog out there on any given day—especially as our previously isolated communities become increasingly interconnected in a global community with a much larger population. This means there is no realistic *best* anymore and any attempt to identify with "being the best" is a glass house waiting to crack.

It is common for people to avoid leaving their comfort zone after they have developed a "winning skill set" in a specific area, even if doing so would be more interesting to them or could provide greater personal meaning. And even for the biggest dog who seems to never lose, they don't get to develop an ability to regulate the personal frustration associated with temporary failure—also called "frustration tolerance." Research studies with college students have shown that *frustration tolerance* is a learned skill directly connected to ongoing motivation in the face of temporary failure, as well as a positive sense of self-esteem and confidence.[41] This means that even for a person who seems to *always* win in competition, they do not learn to develop the *frustration tolerance* required to function adequately outside of their comfort zone—most notably in meaningful social relationships and a rich personal life characteristic to high-quality of life.

2. Man Myth—Emotions interrupt rational thought, so are signs of lacking intelligence and reliability. (The only acceptable emotions are "anger" and sometimes "happy," but only a *little* happy or labeled as "feminine.")

Boys are taught to keep emotions private—even to push emotions below a level of personal conscious awareness—called "denial" or "repression." Emotions do not just disappear when pushed out of the mind, but instead they fester until they are turned either inward into the *internalizing symptoms* like anxiety and depression, or outward into the *externalizing symptoms* of compulsive behavior, anger outbursts or addiction.[42]

Open behavioral expression of physical anger—such as aggression and impulsive anger—is allowed and even encouraged for boys in childhood as a tactic of conflict

---

41   Wang N. (2012) "Study on Frustration Tolerance and Training Method of College Students." In: Liu B., Ma M., Chang J. (eds) *Information Computing and Applications*. ICICA 2012. Lecture Notes in Computer Science, vol 7473. Springer, Berlin, Heidelberg. https://doi.org/10.1007/978-3-642-34062-8_86

42   Ashley, A., and Holtgraves, T. (2003). Repressors and memory: Effects of self-deception, impression management, and mood. *Journal of Research in Personality, 37,* 284–296.

resolution to "settle it on the field [of battle]."[43] Since anger is often associated with toughness and dominance in competition, this emotional experience can usually be openly expressed by men and boys without risk of losing social influence as a result of lacking perceived masculinity.

On a social level, the expression of anger creates a perception of threat to the person across from us—commonly ending in loss of trust, loss of social connection and playing directly into the high rates of social isolation for men.[44] On a more personal level, the experience of anger towards the self results in poor *frustration tolerance*, blocks access to a full range of emotional intelligence, increases perceived threats to self and results in lower motivation to respect the other people involved. Anger does have some important uses that we will discuss later, but it is hardly a sufficient replacement for all of the other emotions that are also a part of the natural human experience.

Instead of experiencing the full breadth of emotions, boys are taught that a "real man" should keep their emotions private. This creates "shame" about the experience of emotions themselves, which only creates a feedback loop of ongoing and compounding pain involved with emotional avoidance.[45] This limitation and systemic blocking of emotional experiences severely limits men from finding personal meaning in their own lives, as well as blocks meaningful intimate relationships with others, friends, family members, and community members alike.

---

43   DiGiuseppe, R., and Tafrate, R. C. (2003). Anger treatment for adults: A meta-analytic review. *Clinical Psychology: Science and Practice, 10*, 70-84.

44   Sorolla, R. G., Russell, P. S. (2019) Not Just Disgust: Fear and Anger Also Relate to Intergroup Dehumanization. *Collabra: Psychology, 5*(1): 56. doi: https://doi.org/10.1525/collabra.211

45   Kaufman, G. (1974). The meaning of shame: Toward a self-affirming identity. *Journal of Counseling Psychology, 21*, 568–574.

3. Man Myth—A "real man" is strong and courageous, as shown by an absence of fear or pain.

Sometimes boys are allowed to express their fear openly, but this is judged as less acceptable the further we get into adulthood and one of the primary reasons that men tend to have fewer close friends than women.[46] Realistically, fear is a natural response to a potential threat and pain is a natural response to immediate harm. An expectation that any human being should never express fear or pain is not only unrealistic but unhealthy, because it blocks people from important feedback about the safety of their environment and essential social needs—both of which are important for survival.

This belief from traditional manhood that men must avoid showing fear or pain again serves well on the battlefield and on the hunt, but beyond these specific settings, it only compounds the shame and avoidance of a man who already believes emotional experiences are an indicator of their stupidity by adding "weak" to the mix! Many boys literally hear the message in childhood, to, *"Come back when you are ready to talk like a man!"* which of course means that social acceptance will be withheld until vulnerable emotions are pushed below the surface.

4. Man Myth—A "real man" is independent and doesn't ask for help.

Boys are taught that the more we can be successful *independently*, the more this shows a high level of personal influence that *nobody* can take away. Meanwhile, asking for

46   Keddie A. (2003). Little boys: Tomorrow's macho lads. *Discourse: Studies in the Cultural politics of Education, 24*(3), 289-306. doi:10.1080/0159630032000172498

help is generally seen as a sign of stupidity, weakness, and/or dependence.

This becomes a severely limiting factor for engaging in needed healthcare because altogether, this combines multiple limiting myths in one place. Engaging in healthcare requires requesting help from another person and the open expression of pain. It doesn't matter that the person helping is a healthcare provider, it is still seen as a sign of dependence and weakness. When it comes to seeking mental healthcare for men, this adds another one of these myths on the pile because the emotional pain is "not rational"—leaving many men feeling *whiny, weak, and stupid.*

This expectation of extreme independence is also prohibitive of optimal team problem solving and sharing meaning through mutual cooperation, which are both requirements of effective leadership, not to mention healthy relationships for a very social species.

5. Man Myth—If violence is needed to "get the job done," then a man must accept the use of violence as "an acceptable means to an end."

As boys, we are not (usually) taught to go out looking for violence, but we *are* taught that a "real man" *never* backs down from a fight. That old advice of, "If that other boy starts it, then you finish it," is usually one of our first lessons in how to respond to social conflict. There is certainly a time and place for using physical leverage to protect oneself and others, but violence is the lowest form of communication and should be avoided until there are no other options.

Young boys are often taught from a young age to "go punch a pillow" to manage anger in the moment. Although this is better than violence towards others or property destruction, a habit formed around this type of instruction creates an expectation for the mind and body that there *will* be a violent physical outlet for emotional tension, whether there is a pillow available for punching—or not. In cases where boys are encouraged to *only* practice expressing a physical outlet for their anger, it is more likely that they become focused on this type of release as the only method for relieving anger. And if anger is the only emotion that men are societally *allowed* to feel, and violence is the only acceptable outlet for that anger, then it should be no surprise that violence is all too common in our society. It is also easy to see why many men are more likely to come off as "controlling" and "irritable" when emotional. Rather than learning how to use a full range of emotions as a guide for personal decision-making that can support navigating social environments productively, men are pigeonholed into a small range of "acceptable" responses.

This overreliance on violence as a central tool for conflict resolution is a set-up for social failure and violence towards self and others. The relative risk of violence from men compared to women in modern society is staggering—even a bit *scary*. Between 1982 and February of 2020, statistics show that out of 114 mass shootings in the United States, 111 of those were by male shooters. In 2012, men accounted for 80% of all violent crimes,[47] but the violence is not just directed outwards to the people around us. It is also directed to *ourselves*! Even though women are more likely to attempt suicide, men have been found to be four *times* as likely to complete suicide worldwide. We must address the root causes of this anger to extricate ourselves from this dangerous and violent situation that we find ourselves in.

---

47   US Department of Justice (2013). Uniform crime report: *crime in the United States 2012. Retrieved from https://ucr.fbi.gov/crime-in-the-u.s/2012/ crime-in-the-u.s.-2012/tables/42tabledatadecoverviewpdf/tab42datadec.pdf*

6. Man Myth—A "real man" should avoid "being/acting like a girl"

"Acting like a girl" is seen as a sign of "weakness" and leaves men vulnerable to losing social status. These feminine traits are rarely defined specifically but are rather understood as the traits "opposite" to those described in numbers 1-5 above. While a "real man" is expected to be competitive, stoic, courageous, independent, and violent, "women" are supposed to be collaborative, emotional, weak, dependent, and subservient. It also includes character traits and skills like compassion, collaboration, patience, and caretaking. The professional roles traditionally associated with femininity incorporate these "female traits" with low pay and low social influence, like teaching, nursing, and administrative support.

This creates social pressure for men to avoid these character traits, interpersonal skills, and professions because they are seen as "feminine," even though they are naturally-occurring qualities of human nature and important roles in a community. Since the "masculine qualities" are highly valued by traditional manhood for securing social influence and self-esteem, the opposite traits are generally devalued.

Even though many men have a natural predisposition for these character traits and/or professional roles, men rarely explore them to our fullest potential because they are devalued as *feminine*.[48] A common outcome here is *lack of personal fulfillment* in our own day-to-day life because there is more of a desire to "look successful, independent and strong," rather than use our natural talents and passions to meaningfully serve our community, or even satisfy basic needs for social connection

48   Juvonen, J., Wang, Y., and Espinoza, G. (2011). Bullying experiences and compromised academic performance across middle school grades. *The Journal of Early Adolescence, 31*(1), 152–173. doi:10.1177/0272431610379415

as a human being. Even when men become very proficient in their professional roles, it is more common for men to struggle with burnout, a lack of satisfaction outside of our professional work, and even chronic health issues as a direct result of the never ending stress associated with being blocked from our full humanity in daily life.

There are so many amazing parts of being a man, but these rigid social and cultural pressures to rely solely on the beliefs and behaviors from traditional manhood encourage social isolation, create chronic health issues, and are even a set-up for unnecessary violence when they are relied on too heavily. This overreliance is what gets people into trouble. Instead we should all aim to integrate the full range of human emotions into our lives, giving the "manly traits" relatively smaller and therefore more balanced roles in our social repertoire.

How Do Boys and Men Learn These Behavioral Expectations and Belief Systems?

Boys learn to rely too heavily on these behaviors and beliefs from traditional manhood largely in our personal experiences in childhood. At the same time, every human being (men included) has different experiences regarding the unique family and community culture that shapes their own personal identity to some degree. While there is some shared similarity amongst men regarding their masculine identity from the myths outlined above, influence from a unique family and community culture also has its own impacts. By looking at these social and cultural forces that compose the rest of personal identity, each person can create the space required to explore their own *unique* self-identity.

The gender specific expectations begin before birth as each family prepares their household for entrance of a new baby.

These gender expectations are largely shaped by caretakers and other significant adults who have beliefs about how their child should be treated and behave. After birth, infants begin to make their own distinctions between boys and girls, as well as assign certain meanings to being male or female based on their own gender socialization experiences.[49] As a child grows up, their gender identity becomes clearer until it eventually has a significant influence on behavior in its own right. In addition to a foundation from traditional gender expectations, each community and family has their own *unique* cultural heritage that creates another set of expectations *inside* the home.

Children are socialized by family through copying parent and sibling behaviors, but there are many other factors at play once a child begins to participate in the surrounding community. These other influences for *socialization* include friends through mimicking behaviors and interests, peers through pressure to uphold group norms and avoid peer rejection, and our greater society through how the media portrays gender expectations. In this process of growing up in today's day and age, people would be expected to have not just one or two, but several different layers of unique interests and values based on their own personal experiences with these competing forces. While variety is the spice of life, significant problems arise when these forces slowly chip away at—even break the spirit of young and developing human beings—who are then only left with expectations of whatever social norms are available to function in daily life.

Studies are showing that the more men and boys have a chance to experience alternative mindsets outside of prescribed roles from traditional manhood with a *unique* family culture,

---

49   David, B., Grace, D. and Ryan, M. (2006). The gender wars: A self categorisation theory perspective on the development of gender identity. In M. Bennet and F. Sani (Eds.), *The development of the social self* (pp.135-157). Hove, UK: Psychology Press.

the better they are able to combat the trappings of those gender expectations in the long run. Boys of color who are introduced to more of their cultural roots show an increase in future planning, prosocial behavior, more active community involvement, as well as lower rates of conviction for criminal behavior in the community as adults.[50] In addition to boys and men of color having better outcomes into adulthood, white men also have a lot to gain from exploring their unique cultural roots.

Men who identify as "white" and are not currently living in Europe like (in the United States or Australia, for instance) have a set of unique cultural roots from a nation of European origin that is not usually central to their personal identity. Whether our ancestors were some of the original English colonists seeking opportunity and freedom from an oppressive monarchy, or the waves of Italians and Irish attracted by plentiful jobs building early American infrastructure, or even Jews seeking safety from the waves of genocide in Europe—all people who can identify as "white" also have their own cultures from nations of origin that are all too easy to forget for some reasons to be discussed in a moment.

This might come as a surprise to learn with all of the recent sociopolitical attention around privilege and oppression, but white men—especially those aged 25-64—are at least *twice* as likely to take their own lives as men in every other racial group except Native Americans, who come in second place for suicide completions behind white men by about 15%. In total, white

---

50   Grills, C., Cooke, D., Douglas, J., Subica, A., Villanueva, S., and Hudson, B. (2016). Culture, racial socialization, and positive African American youth development. *Journal of Black Psychology, 42*(4), 343–373. https://doi.org/10.1177/0095798415578004

males, who make up about 30% of the population, account for nearly 70% of all suicides.[51]

This is hard to see for many healthcare practitioners, so why would we assume that the everyday community member with no medical training will understand the subtle power of these forces? In short, most people cannot see these compounding and often invisible pressures facing men today—including most men themselves. After all, it is much easier for people to choose the path of least resistance because, well, it appears to be more functional and less painful!

While it appears that exposing boys to alternate cultural experiences to traditional manhood are essential for enriching the belief systems and behavioral expectations of boys and men in the long run, the resulting unique viewpoints are commonly another source of tension for boys and men in the short-term—making their long-term value easy to miss. The more there is a difference between expectations for behavior *inside* the home and *outside* the home—and the more these differ from the *natural states* for a child—the more likely these differences will create contact points of tension for personality development called "gender role conflict."

Gender role conflict can be defined more generally as the problems that come from sticking to the traditional expectations of one's gender so rigidly that this restricts, devalues, and even violates the basic rights of self and/or others.[52]

51   Centers for Disease Control and Prevention (2010). Leading cause of deaths in males United States 2010. Retrieved from https://www.cdc.gov/healthequity/lcod/ men/2010/index.htm
52   O'Neil, J. M. (2015). Men's gender role conflict: Psychological costs, consequences, and an agenda for change. Washington, DC: American Psychological Association.

Gender role conflict happens when kids have experiences that tell them their authentic self-identity (outside of traditional gender expectations) is a barrier for meeting basic wants and needs in the environment. In these cases, boys often "overcompensate," or react to the gender role conflict with even *more intense* traditional manhood markers (*aggression, independence, emotional restriction,* etc.) to protect underlying insecurities and fears that are believed to be unacceptable or unworthy of social acceptance. The walls men build to protect themselves and loved ones actually create a prison of their own making.

When a child experiences gender role conflict, caregivers may notice "something is different" with their child that is creating social tension for them. Often they respond with "social policing" to provide "extra support" in the form of social pressure for conforming to preferred social and cultural expectations. Studies have shown that this *policing* from caregivers tends to not only be ineffective for changing any gender expression in question, but also directly creates emotional damage to a child through learning to push down—or "repress"—parts of authentic self. This allows a child to avoid painful social rejection, but at the cost of adopting a personal belief that their true self is unworthy of social acceptance as a human being. Beyond damage done to emotional health and personality development, studies show that *social policing* from caregivers also decreases trust of a child in the caretaking relationship itself that unless resolved, will be extended to a general lack of trust in other people and relationships as an adult.[53]

The pressures of *social policing* are also found inside relationships with peers. Boys who step outside of their given

53   Hill, D. B., and Menvielle, E. (2009). "You have to give them a place where they feel protected and safe and loved": The views of parents who have gender-variant children and adolescents. *Journal of LGBT Youth, 6*(2-3), 243-271. doi:10.1080/19361650903013527

community/family culture have been found to have more experiences with verbal and physical abuse from peers (think "extreme bullying") that may lead to an increase in mental health problems, self-injury, and risk of suicide.[54] Whether the pressure is from family at home or peers in the community, *social policing* is rarely if ever effective in changing a child's true nature.

If anything, this pressure to conform to traditional gender roles only compounds the damage around any existing insecurities resulting from their experience of *gender role conflict*—quite the opposite of "setting them up for success." Regardless, all people are first and foremost human beings with basic social needs *so strong* that most will choose to push down and repress authentic parts of self that represent risk of criticism or rejection until below conscious awareness. Their experiences with *social policing* create a personal belief that these parts of self are unworthy of social acceptance, love, and connection with our most important social groups.

Once these aspects of personal identity are internalized as unworthy of love, a person learns to push those parts of self below the surface to defend from social rejection, but at the cost of self-esteem and personality development. In reality, it is impossible for most men to be "100% manly" at all times by adhering to all of the expectations for traditional manhood[55] without fail—and *especially* in the dynamic roles required by

---

54   Kosciw, J.R., Greytak, E. A., Giga, N. M., Villenas, C., and Danischewiski, D. J. (2016). The 2015 National School Climate Survey: The experiences of lesbian, gay, bisexual, and transgender youth in our nation's schools. New York, NY: GLSEN. Retrieved from https://www.glsen.org/sites/default/files/2015%20National%20 GLSEN%202015%20National%20School%20Climate%20Survey%20%28NSCS%29%20-%20Full%20Report_0.pdf
55   Pleck, J. H. (1995). The gender role strain paradigm: An update. In R. F. Levant and W. S. Pollack (Eds.), A new psychology of men (pp. 11–32). New York, NY: Basic Books

modern society—as opposed to the more traditional and rigid roles of the isolated farming communities once characteristic of the Old World.

This process of gender identity development takes place over time as personal experiences unfold through a child's life, but with a noteworthy emphasis on the formative childhood years. Sometimes there is very clear and direct guidance around what is acceptable versus not acceptable from a child's immediate environments, but even more important than what people say are the personal experiences a child has with the people in those environments.

Many men tend to share similarities around what they would consider masculine identity and this is no surprise, given a shared process of socialization from traditional manhood. But even though many similarities exist, each man also has a unique self-identity because no two family histories or set of personal experiences will be exactly alike.

Even though this might *sound* very natural and reasonable, that no two men have the same *exact* identity regarding their masculinity, these unique identity developments for each man tend to create their own problems. These problems come from points of tension between these unique parts of true self and the social pressure to adhere to traditional manhood expectations— or face the very real risk of social rejection. These sources of *gender role conflict* create barriers for many men when it comes to personal life satisfaction, general health, as well as the quality of personal relationships.

There has been a lot of recent attention from critical social movements like the Me Too Movement, Black Lives Matter and Gay Pride about sexism harming women, racism harming people of color, and homophobia harming LGBTQ+ identifying people. In fact, the social and political agendas from these movements have appeared to target men and their *male privilege* inherited from the Old World as central to the problem.

This attempt by feminist movements to protect vulnerable community members might be well-intended, but this type of approach tends to stimulate the defenses of many men because it can easily seem like a personal attack. This defensive stance typically results in a reliance on the same old belief systems and behavior expectations from the Old World to protect their social and cultural viewpoints from a perceived assault on personal identity. Rather than each group learning more about the other to gain each other's trust and cooperate towards shared goals, this type of approach only serves to reinforce tribal lines and polarize the social and cultural agendas of each "side"—as was evident in many ways leading up to the 2016 and 2020 United States presidential elections.

Many people, even seasoned academics and practitioners from psychology and sociology, are surprised to learn that most men and boys face *gender role conflict* that results in limitations to personal well-being in exchange for accessing the social influence available through *male privilege.* Since it *is* "A Man's World" in so many different ways, aren't all men just fat and happy? The short answer is "No," and in fact, the pressure from social oppression is hurting *all* community members—men and boys included.

The combined fatality statistics for men show that deaths by drug overdose, alcohol toxicity, and suicide together—a category aptly named "deaths of despair" —have been rising significantly over the last few decades. The mortality rate from deaths of despair *far* surpasses anything seen in America since the beginning of the 1900s—especially for men! This sharp increase since 1999 has been primarily driven by an unprecedented epidemic of drug overdoses, but even excluding those deaths, the combined mortality rate from suicides and alcohol-related deaths is higher than at *any* point in more than 100 years. Suicides have not been so common since 1938 (World War II), and one has to go back to the 1910s to find mortality rates from alcohol-related deaths (the Prohibition Era) that are as high as those found today.[56]

The qualities of traditional manhood are quite effective on the battlefield and while on a hunt, but under the dynamic interpersonal pressures of daily life in modern society—these traditional belief systems and behavior expectations are not sustainable in terms of quality of life or even lifespan. In fact, the increase in average lifespan over the last century is drastically shorter for men and boys when compared to our female peers.

In 1920, life expectancy at birth for females was only two years greater than for males. By year 2000, the female advantage was up to six years, when life expectancy was seventy-four for males and eighty for females.[57] Men's health statistics show that men are struggling with chronic illness, self-neglect (as defined by failure to access available preventative healthcare), and addiction to illicit drugs at significantly higher rates than women—not to mention a suicide rate that is four *times* higher than that of women worldwide.[58] Despite men having some socioeconomic advantages by earning roughly 20% more than

56   Long-Term trends in deaths of despair (2019, September 5). United States Congress Joint Economic Committee. Retrieved April 8, 2021 from https://www.jec.senate.gov/public/index.cfm/republicans/2019/9/long-term-trends-in-deaths-of-despair

57   A.M. Minino et al., "Deaths: Final Data for 2000," *National Vital Statistics Reports* 50, no. 15 (2002); Ian P.F. Owens, "Sex Differences in Mortality Rates," *Science*, 297 (September 20, 2002): 2008-2009.

58   DeLeo, D., Draper, B.M., Snowdon, J.,and Kolves, K. (2013). Contacts with health professionals before suicide: Missed opportunities for prevention. *Comprehensive Psychiatry.* 54(7), 1117-1123. doi:10.1016/j.comppsych.2013.06.007

women for the same work[59], the age-adjusted death rate has shown to be at least 40% higher for men than for women.[60]

In fact, studies show the more men stick to the behavioral expectations and belief systems characteristic of traditional manhood that encourages "toughing it out" independently in the face of pain without asking for help, the less access to adequate support is available and as a result, men become more chronically stressed—eventually resulting in mental and physical illness.[61] Men and boys might get to reap the spoils of war in this "man's world" for the short-term, but doing so with the tools available from traditional manhood only separates men from their authentic self-identity and from meaningful long-term relationships with others—the two factors most closely connected to life satisfaction for human beings.[62]

Unless men learn to integrate the rest of their humanity into self-identity, a rigid adherence to the behavioral expectations and belief systems of traditional manhood separates them from the more social parts of life that are incredibly important for human beings as a species—both men and women alike. These belief systems and behavioral expectations of traditional manhood not only create physical health problems, but also lead many men down a path of poor mental health and isolation—

---

59   McIntosh, P. (2007). White privilege and male privilege: A personal account of coming to see correspondence through work in women's studies. In M. L. Andersen & P. H. Collins (Eds.), *Race, class, and gender: An anthology* (6th ed.). Belmont, CA: Wadsworth.
60   Hoyart, D. L., and Xu, J. (2012) Deaths: Preliminary data for 2011. *National Vital Statistics Reports*, 61, 1-52. Retrieved from http://www.cdc.gov/nchs/data/nvsr/nvsr61/nvser61_06.pdf
61   Addis, M. E. (2008). Gender and depression in men. *Clinical Psychology: Science and Practice*, 15(3), 153-168. doi:10.1111/j.1468-2850.2008.00125.x
62   Vaillant, G., Mukamal K. Successful Aging. *American Journal of Psychiatry*, 2001: 158:839-847

even becoming unfair, aggressive, and violent towards other community members and themselves.

It is easy to see how men get a lot of reinforcement for upholding these expectations of traditional manhood, even if they are a detriment to health. You would be hard-pressed to see a man receive criticism for showing unending enthusiasm for climbing the corporate ladder, avoiding emotional expression or being known as someone that "you shouldn't mess with or else." These behavioral expectations and belief systems for men provide useful tools for navigating the immediate demands of daily life successfully, but all too easily become dependent on these tactics when they are believed to be the only methods available. In reality, an over reliance on these behaviors and belief systems teaches men to obsessively use these tactics *in all situations* because of the effectiveness they appear to have in the short-term and a perceived lack of alternate options for thoughts, feelings, and behaviors to navigate the stressors of daily life.

For instance, anxiety symptoms often develop when someone becomes hyperfocused on coercive control because to them, they "have to stay two steps ahead" by controlling the outcome to remain secure in their own position. Sometimes it goes in the other direction with depression symptoms when a man sees that it is impossible for him to uphold these behaviors and belief systems at all times—so he develops a state of "learned helplessness," a condition found in not only humans with depression, but also many other animals in cases where they learn that no matter what, there will be unavoidable failure so there is no point in even trying.[63, 64]

63   Seligman, M. E. (1974). *Depression and learned helplessness.* In R. J. Friedman and M. M. Katz (Eds.), *The psychology of depression: Contemporary theory and research.* John Wiley and Sons.
64   Forgeard, M. J., Haigh, E. A., Beck, A. T., Davidson, R. J., Henn, F. A., Maier, S. F., Mayberg, H. S., and Seligman, M. E. (2011). Beyond Depression:

There are also many cases where coercive behavior towards other people in the immediate environment continues to escalate until it becomes aggressive and even violent. More public awareness around the use of coercive—even violent behavior— by men towards women and less powerful men recently came to a head with the Me Too Movement, where social media provided a platform for many celebrities to openly state that "they too" had been the victims of sexual and dating violence.[65]

Traditional manhood behaviors and belief systems still serve important functions in some parts of life for modern society (e.g., the military), but problems start to happen when these expectations from the Old World are maintained too rigidly or get combined with each other in a way that results in compounded gender role conflict that creates barriers for meeting basic needs as human beings—at times even blocking others from meeting their own.

It is also important to remember that as a global community, human beings now have a WIDE range of different cultural groups left over from the isolated farming communities of the Old World—all with their own behaviors, appearance, language, customs, etc. These social and cultural practices not only helped maintain a degree of social cohesion and order in the Old World, but have also provided methods for identifying "outsiders" who posed a threat to our community of "insiders" as "the other." This happened first in the hunter-gatherer societies early in our evolution, then became even more pronounced in the isolated farming communities.

Towards a Process-Based Approach to Research, Diagnosis, and Treatment. Clinical psychology: a publication of the Division of Clinical Psychology of the American Psychological Association, 18(4), 275–299. https://doi.org/10.1111/ j.1468-2850.2011.01259.x

65   "From Politics to Policy: Turning the Corner on Sexual Harassment—Center for American Progress." *Center for American Progress.* January 31, 2018.

The protector role has been central to male identity since the beginning of time, but this role must now be updated well beyond the use of physical aggression to immediately neutralize any perceived threat to law and order. Without an update for modern society, this easily becomes an automatic reaction to objectify and/or display aggressive behavior towards the perceived "other" that many now share a community with, or even females and other vulnerable community members if that is what is required "to neutralize the threat."

The tribal nature of human beings is a "double-edged sword." People must have meaningful connections with other people to be healthy and happy. But at the same time, the tribal drive to dehumanize outsiders as "the other" will be our demise if it continues to go unchecked as we undergo this transition to a global community. We must learn as a society to transition out of those primitive roots and evolve past those ancient and outdated demands.

You might have heard the popular phrase of "the melting pot" that is often used to describe the culturally-diverse urban communities that have become more characteristic of modern society since the Industrial Revolution. There is certainly more diversity in urban spaces as a whole when compared to isolated farming communities, but the available resources are NOT evenly "melted," or distributed, which creates issues for the health of this system of interdependent relationships—also called an "ecosystem."

A primary agent for driving the ongoing health of an ecosystem comes from "natural selection"—a phrase popularized first by Charles Darwin,[66] then later tweaked with the addition

---

[66]   *Darwin, Charles, 1809-1882. (1859). On the origin of species by means of natural selection, or preservation of favoured races in the struggle for life. London :John Murray*

of genetics and "Law of Inheritance" from Gregory Mendel[67] to create our modern understanding of evolutionary biology.[68] This process has been briefly described up to this point to explain the historical context for how human beings developed from apes over millions of years, as well as how the functional adaptations have created a set of basic needs that is unique and essential to our species.

For a process of *natural selection* to occur, there must be freely flowing resources. This allows a maintenance of sustainable and healthy processes for an ecosystem to self-regulate by letting go of what is no longer functional, while also remaining flexible and open to more adaptive ways of functioning. This promotes increased mastery over the environment so that animals (in this case people) who are most successful in a given environment are most likely to create offspring who will continue this trend of success for the species.

If we look at urban communities and now the global community, the human race is more of a chunky stew that is far from a harmonious and sustainable mixture of its different parts. These pockets of greater density are largely functions of coercive power used by colonizing forces of the Old World, rather than as a result of having adaptive social and economic function of a healthy system governed by natural selection. Any limitation on the freedom of resource flow serves to create unequal distribution, which blocks the ability of the system to self-regulate—both inside of each individual, between each other in social relationships, as well as inside the institutions that are charged with supporting our communities.

---

67   Butler, John M. (2010). *Fundamentals of Forensic DNA Typing.* Burlington, MA: Elsevier/Academic Press. pp. 34–35. ISBN 978-0-08-096176-7.

68   Ellis, T.H. Noel; Hofer, Julie M.I.; Timmerman-Vaughan, Gail M.; Coyne, Clarice J.; Hellens, Roger P. (2011). "Mendel, 150 years on." *Trends in Plant Science.* 16 (11): 590–96. doi:10.1016/j.tplants.2011.06.006

This is where it gets interesting because despite what many people might assume, those who "rise to the top" with minimal barriers do not "have it made". In reality, a process of inorganic access to resources harms these individuals as well—it is just below the obvious surface level.

Most men are taught as boys to become overreliant on the behaviors and belief systems available from traditional manhood. As a result, those men get compulsively focused on, or "addicted to," the leverage provided by these behaviors and belief systems that have become markers of social status in the form of "male privilege."

Once someone creates a habit of using these tactics to gain mastery in their environment, it becomes a lot more difficult to release the associated thoughts, feelings, and behaviors. Sometimes these habits even remain out of conscious awareness entirely (called "compulsive" or "obsessive"). When this happens, these unconscious habits form a load-bearing wall of the "ego" that the person considers vital to their roles, responsibilities, and personal identity.

Once behaviors and belief systems from traditional manhood become more and more ingrained with prolonged use, the ego flags any parts of authentic self-identity that do not match the traditional social codes as taboo. As a result, those clashing traits are pushed into unconscious awareness ("repressed") and understood by the person (both consciously and unconsciously) as unsuitable for use and/or personal identification. In this case, a person believes that to act in such a way would risk being labeled, "unworthy of social acceptance."

Case Study: Michael was a professional executive who came to me seeking treatment for ongoing "relationship issues" and perhaps most notably, his habit of becoming possessive, and even aggressive, with romantic partners. Michael grew up in a home where one parent used the same controlling and abusive tactics towards him, which resulted in his being shy and untrusting socially. The local bullies picked up on Michael's lack of confidence and identified him as an easy target, where he had ongoing experiences of acute social bullying that compounded those wounds. He was also bright and handsome, so soon got the attention of young women once he was of dating age. Michael really appreciated this positive attention and was even more delighted when he realized that having a girlfriend made the bullies less likely to attack him. This seemed to go very well until Michael became obsessed and possessive over his girlfriends, associating them with the only safety and affection he had ever known. This culminated in a domestic assault charge that brought him into my office.

It is almost as if there is an "invisible electric fence" that keeps men in a relatively small area of available strategies all derived from traditional manhood. This leads many men to become hyperfocused, even compulsive, in using these unfair practices for social influence. And while the user sometimes has conscious awareness of being confined by these limiting beliefs, the personal barriers almost always remain out of conscious awareness because they are woven into cultural training and social practices so thoroughly. This makes these behaviors and belief systems feel "normal/familiar," which in turn makes them very difficult to recognize as limiting factors in and of themselves.

While all men tend to have these limiting factors of traditional manhood in common to some degree, men are also granted a degree of social and political influence compared to women. This relatively "invisible" *male privilege* has real impacts on how our society functions.

For example, prior to the Affordable Care Act of 2010, health insurance policies frequently excluded coverage for prenatal care and childbirth.[69] Ensuring healthy babies is something that all societies benefit from and surely providing insurance coverage to access needed resources would help that goal. But realistically only women get pregnant and give birth and very few women run insurance companies.

Male dominance is similar in the corporate world, where the thirty-two women who led Fortune 500 companies in 2017 accounted for only 6.4% of all Fortune 500 CEOs.[70] Thus corporate culture has, for many years, awarded traditionally male traits. Those who are hyper-competitive, ruthless, and brash are promoted, while those that are sheepish or ask for time off to spend with their families are not.

The world of politics paints a similar picture. In 2018, only twenty-two of the one hundred American senators were female and the eighty-four women in the House of Representatives made up 19.3% of that body. Out of fifty state governors, only six of them were female at this time (12% of total), while women made up slightly more than 25% of state legislators.[71] The men in these positions, while purportedly working for the entire

---

69   Kodjak, Alison. "GOP Health Bill Changes Could Kill Protections For Those With Pre-Existing Conditions." March 23, 2017 https://www.npr.org/sections/health-shots/2017/03/23/521220359/gop-health-bill-changes-could-kill-protections-forpeople-with-preexisting-condi

70   Zarya, Valentina. "The 2017 Fortune 500 Includes a Record Number of Women CEOs." June 7, 2017. http://fortune. com/2017/06/07/fortune-women-ceos/

71   "Women in State Legislatures 2018" Center for American Women and Politics, Rutgers http://www.cawp.rutgers.edu/ women-state-legislature-2018

population, have instead continuously promoted policies that pprotect and enhance male dominance in modern society.

The gender pay gap is narrowing, with women in the U.S. now making $0.83 on the dollar that is earned by men. [72] This is partially a result of women having more pressure to take time off of their jobs to raise children, which negatively affects their earning potential. Women also tend to cluster in lower paying jobs such as teaching, nursing, and social work. But have you ever considered *why* these professions come with lower pay? The roles of teaching the youth of our future and healing our sick are certainly important professional roles in any community. The inevitable conclusion is that these professions are paid less, because men have historically had the power to set wages and women make up the majority of workers in these roles. [73]

Male privilege also reveals itself in hiring and compensation practices for the same professions. A 2012 Yale study looked at identical resumes for their professors, finding that *both* male and female science professors were more likely to hire male support staff. Further, the men's salaries were $4,000 more annually than female peers with the exact same positions. [74]

The aforementioned statistics present the current state of imbalance between the relative economic and political positions of influence held by men versus women in present times. Given its effective use for social influence, it is difficult for most men

72   Brown, Anna and Patten, Eileen. "The narrowing, but persistent, gender gap in pay." Pew Research Center. April 3, 2017 http://www.pewresearch.org/fact-tank/2017/04/03/gender-pay-gap-facts/
73   Cain Miller, Claire. "As Women Take Over a Male-Dominated Field, the Pay Drops." The New York Times. March 18, 2016. https://www.nytimes.com/2016/03/20/upshot/as-women-take-over-a-male-dominated-field-the-pay-drops.html
74   "Scientist not immune from gender bias, Yale study shows." YaleNews. September 24, 2012. https://news.yale.edu/2012/09/24/scientists-not-immune-gender-bias-yale-study-shows

to consider giving up the short-term incentives available from *male privilege*. Beyond earning potential, this also includes the availability of personal choices to (temporarily) avoid the painful reality of emotional and physical pain as a "show of strength," have the "final say" when it comes to important family/community decision-making as the primary protector, and even avoid accountability for coercion and violence if an argument can be made that the intention is to protect someone from a perceived threat. To put it clearly, a man can only wield the attractive short-term benefits of male privilege when he is also willing to repress the development and maintenance of his own humanity in the process.[75]

This might be hard to understand at first glance because again, many people who cannot see all of the layers involving gender norms will assume that since there is an imbalance of social influence between men and women, that those with more social influence are the "winners," while those with less social influence must be the clear "losers" since they have less access to community resources. This blanket assumption would argue that when it comes to male privilege, that men are always the winners and women are always the losers. Even though this is a common assumption by much of the "feminist movement,"[76,77] health outcome statistics actually paint a very different picture.

Rather than being beneficial, use of male privilege as taught tends to come at a great hidden cost. It is easy to forget that the user of the social influence available from male privilege must also adhere to the strict brief systems and behavioral expectations that govern the social and cultural guidelines for

75   O'Neil, J. M., and Renzulli, S. (2013). Introduction to the special section: Teaching the psychology of men: A call to action. *Psychology of Men and Masculinity, 14*(3), 221–229. doi:10.1037/a0033258
76   Friedan, Betty. (1963). The feminine mystique. New York: Norton.
77   Solnit, R., and Fernandez, A. T. (2014). *Men explain things to me.* Chicago: Haymarket Books.

traditional manhood.[78] This requires the user to push down, or "repress," their own personal identity, emotional experiences, and basic social needs until the needs are below conscious awareness. The only blueprints allowed to remain in conscious awareness are the belief systems and behavior expectations from traditional manhood, because these strategies are the only ones with a track record of success. But while the results might "look successful," the use of these tactics come at great costs to the user and those around them.

Most importantly, men are not allowed to have a full range of emotional experiences as boys while being taught to "man up," so are rarely taught to master these skills before entering adulthood. This teaches most men to be comfortable with anger (and maybe a little bit of happy), but the other emotional experiences become taboo as representing a very real risk of social rejection. As a result, they get pushed out of conscious awareness until many men cannot even consciously identify them.

Thus when men face a challenging situation, there is a sense of fear and insecurity about the emotional experiences themselves on *top* of the acute situation. In a state of stress all people revert to their familiar behaviors, which ultimately blocks many men from learning to regulate emotional experiences and the accompanying physiological arousal that naturally occurs in response to stressors. But the more people learn to navigate a full range of emotional experiences that come "pre-packaged" as part of a human being's natural social programming, the better a person becomes at regulating emotional experiences, actively influence related thoughts, and change behavior that is no longer functional in the current context so we can be adaptable and

78   Mankowski, E. S., and Matton, K. I. (2010). A community psychology of men and masculinity: Historical and conceptual review. *American Journal of Community Psychology, 45*(1-2), 73-86. doi:10.1007/s10464-009-9288-y

healthy at the same time.[79] This inability to regulate emotional experiences not only blocks men from their own innate personal wisdom, but also blocks men from meaningful and satisfying relationships with other people.

No matter how tough a protector or proficient of a financial provider a man might become, without loved ones knowing personal thoughts, feelings, and intentions there will never be true intimate connection. Even though conflict can be difficult, it is in times of tension when a relationship is forced to dig deeper to the next level of connection by increasing understanding and trust, or grow stagnant—sometimes even taking the shape of mere affiliation more typical of "roommates." In fact, a man's adherence to these standards of traditional manhood have been positively associated with their wife's depression,[80] as well as parenting concerns and work-family conflict.[81]

As you might imagine, a surface level relationship—no matter how sexy, exciting, and lust-filled—is not likely to last over time. For a long-term relationship to survive, romantic partners must grow beyond the initial stages of lust by creating a relationship based on safety and security. This experience of deep connection releases a brain chemical required for social bonding called "oxytocin." While this feels pleasant, it is very different from the intoxicating brain chemical of "dopamine"— the "feel good chemical" characteristic of pleasure that is

79   Liu, W. M. (2005). The study of men and masculinity as an important multicultural competency consideration. *Journal of Clinical Psychology, 61*(6), 685-697. doi: 10.1002/jlcp.20103

80   Breidin, M. J., Windle, C. R., and Smith, D. A. (2008). Interspousal criticism: A behavioral mediator between husbands' gender role conflict and wives' adjustment. *Sex Roles, 59*(11-12), 880-888. doi:10.1007/s11199-008-9491-6

81   Fouad, N. A., Whiston, S. C., and Feldwisch, R. (2016). Men and men's careers. In Y. J. Wong, and S. R. Wester (Eds.), *APA handbook of men and masculinities* (pp. 503–524). Washington, DC: American Psychological Association. doi:10.1037/14594-023

dumped into the brain during the "honeymoon phase" of a romantic relationship.

Studies show that levels of dopamine can be expected to drop by 8% every year for the first seven years of marriage.[82] This means that roughly half of the excitement and passion in a marriage is expected to exit the union in the first decade! Is it a surprise that the current trend over the last 25 years is that roughly half of American couples will get divorced? And that *over* half will get divorced in their second marriage?[83]

At the same time, for men this appears to be a "catch-22." The first option is to openly show loved ones uncomfortable emotions, which seems to be in direct conflict with being seen as strong and capable—generally reliable enough to retain traditional roles of protector and provider. The second option is to push down those vulnerable emotions with the belief that this is "being a nice guy" or "taking one for the team" in the hopes that emotional discomfort will just go away on its own and lifelong satisfaction will develop over time if they "just hang in there."

It really is a choice between two conflicting aspects of personal identity, and either choice involves leaving some aspect of personal identity behind. This creates a significant barrier to intimacy in adult relationships.[84] The divorce statistics clearly show that the state of the modern romantic relationship is in trouble and even though this might sound like the opposite of "common sense" to many men, a large part of the puzzle is *us.*

82   Lieberman, Daniel Z. and Long, Michael E. (2018). *The Molecule of More: How a Single Chemical in Your Brain Drives Love, Sex, and Creativity--and Will Determine the Fate of the Human Race.* BenBella Books

83   Shaw, L.A. (2010). Divorce mediation outcome research: A meta-analysis. *Conflict Resolution Quarterly, 27*(4): 447-467.

84   Pollack, W. S. (1995) No man is an island: Toward a new psychoanalytic psychology of men. In R. F. Levant and W. S. Pollack (Eds.), *A new psychology of men* (pp.33-67). New York, NY: Basic Books.

The habit a emotional avoidance blocks the risk of vulnerability but along with that it blocks the warmth and accessibility that must be experienced by people in a satisfying personal relationship—whether this is a lover, friend, or colleague.

Degrees of intimacy/connection from highest to lowest

1-lover	2-friend	3-colleague	4-acquaintance
unlock each other's growth as "secure base"	can even become "like family"	enough shared values to collaborate towards shared goals outside of the home	how do you think they become friends?

In addition to blocking intimacy and deep connection, a reliance on anger tends to be threatening to other people, resulting in their active withdrawal from a relationship.[85] This pushes people away, making it harder for men to advocate for themselves effectively in a way that others can understand clearly, which is *supposed* to be the basic adaptive function of "speaking up" for human beings.

Unless a person learns to communicate their thoughts feelings and needs to others clearly and respectfully enough, there will be no way to meet these important social needs. And if someone does not manage their behavior when upset in a way that also avoids threatening the needs of others (whether consciously intended while "having an outburst"—or not), then the trust of that community member is lost. Together, this disrupts the ability of men to meet basic social needs by encouraging isolation.

---

85   O'Neill, J. M. (2013). *Men's gender role conflict: Psychological costs, consequences, and agenda for change.* Washington, DC: American Psychological Association.

Since the global pandemic, there has been more of a focus on the impact of social isolation on physical and mental health. The fields of social sciences have understood the importance of social contact on general wellness for decades, but recent evidence from multidisciplinary studies around neuroscience has shown that prolonged social isolation causes ongoing stimulation of our sympathetic nervous system. As we discussed in chapter 2, this releases cortisol, the same stress hormone released when facing a dangerous or stressful situation. Extended cortisol release is associated with anxiety, insomnia, premature aging, autoimmune disease, cardiovascular disease and poor immune health.[86] Thus social isolation puts the same stress on the human body as if weeks were set being chased by a bear.

The sympathetic nervous system is regulated and soothed by the parasympathetic nervous system—also called "rest/digest"—that is stimulated by the release of *oxytocin*. Oxytocin is associated with an experience of "social bonding" that promotes healing, tissue repair/recovery, immune support, and even future testosterone production.[87] With these complementary stress systems of the body in mind, it is easy to see how prolonged social isolation leaves people unable to regulate their stress response, placing a significant amount of unnecessary wear and tear on all the organs of the body.

Sometimes people do not stop at isolating themselves and rather, redirect their personal unhappiness towards the other people around them. Even though the majority of males are not violent, males commit roughly 80% of all violent crimes

86   Heim C, Ehlert U, Hellhammer DH. The potential role of hypocortisolism in the pathophysiology of stress-related bodily disorders. *Psychoneuroendocrinology.* 2000;25:1–35.
87   Vinik AI, Maser RE, Ziegler D. Autonomic imbalance: prophet of doom or scope for hope? *Diabetic Medicine* 2011;28:643–651

in the United States.[88] Since traditional manhood socially and culturally normalizes the use of violence, while at the same time making vulnerable emotional expression taboo, the display of aggression can often serve as social proof of perceived masculinity when this is believed to be under threat in a state of personal insecurity—as discussed earlier in the form of *overcompensation*.[89]

Since men are taught as boys to avoid expressing pain and asking for help, many males keep their injuries and personal needs to themselves, even if the expression of this personal information is required to access needed support. Men achieve this by burying uncomfortable emotions under an extra layer of "shame."

We will discuss emotions, what each of them mean, and how to use them in greater detail later in this book. For now, we will take a brief look at this distinctly male shame that reinforces emotional restriction. *Shame* is the emotional experience generally related to social rejection—that someone is not worthy of acceptance and love. A male's practice of emotional restriction is socially reinforced by the common belief from traditional manhood that open expression of vulnerable emotions will surely result in being rejected from the social status of a "strong man."

This added layer of social reinforcement for emotional restriction creates a layer of shame over ALL emotions, which helps to keep them (especially the vulnerable emotions) frozen

---

88   United States Department of Justice (2011). *Homicide trends in the United States, 1980-2008: Annual rates for 2009 and 2010.* Washington, DC: Bureau of Justice Statistics. Retrieved from http://www.bjs.gov/content/pub/pdf/htus8008.pdf

89   Whitehead, A. (2005) Man to man violence: How masculinity may work as a dynamic risk factor. *The Howard Journal of Criminal Justice, 44*(4), 411-422. doi:10.1111/j.1468-2311.2005.00385.x

beneath the surface and outside of conscious awareness. This layer of shame-supported avoidance serves to protect social status in the short-term, but again this is only a set-up for worsening issues in the long-term. Like any threat to personal safety for humans—social rejection included—this results in the stimulation of the sympathetic nervous system, resulting in a dump of cortisol, which negatively impacts brain health, testosterone production, immune function, cardiovascular health, digestive function, as well as function of the our endocrine system.[90]

In addition to this playing out poorly for the general health and well-being of men in everyday life, shame also blocks men from accessing needed support. This socially and culturally trained belief that all parties are "doing something wrong" by openly expressing and witnessing vulnerability commonly keeps men and boys from even disclosing a painful or traumatic experience, let alone receiving needed medical care to recover.

Recent studies with combat veterans who have PTSD shows that health outcomes are significantly worse for vets who display more of the traditional manhood behaviors and belief systems—placing them at greater risk for both the development of PTSD, as well as the experience of more severe symptoms associated with this condition.[91]

This brief introduction to the current state of men's health shows a clear picture of how the expectations for traditional

90   Yaribeygi, H., Panahi, Y., Sahraei, H., Johnston, T. P., & Sahebkar, A. (2017). The impact of stress on body function: A review. *EXCLI journal, 16*, 1057–1072. https://doi.org/10.17179/excli2017-480

91   Neilson, E. C., Singh, R. S., Harper, K. L., and Teng, E. J. (2020). Traditional Masculinity Ideology, Posttraumatic Stress Disorder (PTSD) Symptom Severity, and Treatment in Service Members and Veterans: A Systematic Review. *Psychology of Men and Masculinities.* Advance online publication. http://dx.doi.org/10.1037/men0000257

manhood are making men ill, as well as placing more vulnerable community members at greater risk. *But how could this be*? Men and women's roles have evolved with each other for thousands of years to complement each other in a family and community setting, so how did everything get out of balance so *quickly*? In many ways, all of these tension points are now becoming more problematic due to the most recent social evolution of mankind—*The Global Community.*

CHAPTER 5: REINTEGRATING HUMANITY FOR HEALING IN MODERN SOCIETY

Between the dramatic increase in global population over the last century and more recent developments in modern technology, people can now connect and share information across the planet rapidly. The isolated farming communities of the Old World are gone. We now live with far greater physical and social proximity than ever before. This shift towards a globally-connected community is a significant development for the social and cultural expectations that have driven human behavior from our early hunting and gathering ancestors, through the farming communities of the Neolithic Revolution, into the Industrial Revolution and up to the present point in time.

In 2020, the global COVID-19 pandemic has shown that a pathogen can physically travel across the Earth in one day—a mere 24 hours. We have had pandemics before, but they were far more localized to specific regions, like the Bubonic Plague in Europe and Ebola in Africa, because physical movement was relatively limited. Now that the capability to travel by plane is so readily available to all corners of the world, a physical pathogen like a virus can spread much more quickly from one region of the world to another.

This recent increase in global population density is a very significant physical development in how humanity inhabits the Earth. This must be taken into careful consideration by global leaders who may need to adjust international practices to provide our communities with the necessary protections. Even countries who have historically enjoyed benefits from more isolationist international policies must now reconsider these responsibilities to our own nation of origin—as well as our global community—if we are to protect ourselves sufficiently as a species.

The other notable shift that has caused an abrupt increase in proximity forming a global community is modern technology. With the push of a button and swipe of a finger, we can access seemingly limitless information about science, history, social issues, and current events. In 1991, the World Wide Web became available to the public and it was only in 2001 that the internet became available on smartphones. Then Apple released the iPhone to the market in 2007, setting off the smartphone revolution. By 2018, at least 2.5 billion people—roughly 35% of the world's population—had access to the world wide web on their cell phone.[92]

Before the internet arrived in 1991, leaders of each community around the world controlled access to information for its own community members in written print—if the community members were even literate. That allowed the leaders of each community to make the choice of either restricting access of information to the "outside world" and blocking it completely, or providing access—depending on the relative needs of the community based on cultural and social practices. It is more common for totalitarian governments to highly censor, if not block access to this information completely, while more democratic governments trend towards greater access.

The importance of this access to information outside of our immediate community cannot be understated for such a social

---

92   Pew Research Center, February 2019, "Smartphone Ownership Is Growing Rapidly Around the World, but Not Always Equally."

species as human beings. Remember, our ways of understanding life as we know it are based on standardized social and cultural expectations that guide belief systems and behavior. For this reason, the leaders in power for each community might view access to information as a necessity for critical thought and personal freedom. Or this new information might appear to be so different from the existing social and political structure that that they believe that it represents a threat to the established order and/or their own power.

As greater numbers of people throughout the world are gaining access to the internet, not only facts but also social trends are able to spread across the globe with the same speed of a virus. Thus the term "viral" for a meme, a trend, a tweet, or a video that spreads around the internet in a matter of hours. Whether we are talking about the latest dance craze to a catchy song, or a more significant shift in belief systems away from racism and homophobia, we are seeing a global pushback against certain social and cultural expectations that have long been a part of the traditional cultural landscape. Even though a global community is beginning to take shape, the social and cultural expectations from the Old World largely remain embedded within the institutions that govern communities in modern society. Like when we are confronted with something that needs to change within ourselves, communities also tend to vehemently resist impending change.

When we take a look at the social and political tensions currently developing throughout the world—like women's rights with the Me Too Movement, internet censorship by totalitarian governments (still a popular approach in some isolationist countries), as well as a global push-back against racism and LGBTQ+ rights—we can see that those movements are happening because community members have lost trust in their leaders. Individuals can now see outside of the limited boundaries of social experience often held in place by the coercive control of leaders that was typical in Old World communities. With our newfound abilities to easily communicate between communities and learn how other communities successfully function, these tactics are being exposed in a rapidly evolving global community. This has naturally resulted in the loss of trust in our leadership by the general public over the years. Our forefathers understood that there should be "no taxation without representation." Now, through our global interconnection, we know that our leaders are ignoring the personal thoughts and opinions of community members regarding important decision making.

Men have been the primary hunters and warriors for our communities because, as with most other mammals, nature has provided men with relative independence from the physical responsibility of childbearing. As a result, men developed powerful physical bodies and have been culturally trained to personally identify with social expectations for the heavy lifting of providing resources and protecting family and community. This has provided men with the opportunity to develop valuable gifts and capabilities, but how are they supposed to use this influence in a way that serves and protects vulnerable community members when the available methods involve self-neglect, extreme independence, and coercion of others to fulfill these roles? As you might imagine, these behaviors and belief systems are much more likely to set the stage for an *erosion* of trust and understanding!

This lack of allowance for human needs to be met in personal relationships can be seen not only in one-on-one interactions between community members, but also in how people are expected to interact with the institutions that govern our communities. The essential human needs of shared meaning and trust have become so absent between community members and our governing institutions that this has left significant gaps in protecting the health and well-being of all people in modern society—men included.

Providing Resources in Modern Society

First, on a level of providing resources, there are far fewer skilled trades full of personal meaning to be passed down through multiple generations of family, like being a carpenter or baker. This means that a man no longer has to adhere to a family trade in order to provide for their family, but can go into the open market as an inexperienced worker. Even if many men were willing to brave the modern markets in a family-owned business, there is rarely an "in-house mentor" or an established book of clients to rely on. Corporate interests swallowed most of the independently-held businesses alive in the mid-19th century, centralizing production of goods, and diverting resources from communities into the pockets of wealthy executives.

The modern marketplace driven by corporations tends to be full of jobs that are highly-specified, repetitive, and rarely require the mastery and skill set commonly found in family trades with skilled craftsmen of the Old World. As a result, most men in modern society have no choice but to get swept up in the everyday demands of big business, especially with the added pressure from a traditional male role as the primary provider.

There are four specific issues in the role of provider for men directly resulting from the recent transitions into a more urban and now globally connected marketplace: less job security, physical/mental health breakdown, no more personal sense of purpose at work, and no more meaningful connection in the workplace as part of a community outside of the home.

No Job Security—Workers are easily replaced because factory operations have become more and more reliant on machines and other automated mechanisms through the years. Human workers are generally only involved to complete specialized, repetitive, and often simple tasks that are not easily automated. Because the tasks rarely require critical thinking, workers can be easily replaced. At the same time, because of the simplicity of the arrangement, the skills are often not transferrable.

This "efficiency-focused" mission of corporate business culture certainly increases productivity in the short-term, but it also cuts most workers off from understanding the "big picture" of how to function independently in their industry. This, in turn, makes it psychologically more difficult for workers to consider striking out on their own. Creating your own business involves using an entrepreneurial skill set that is rarely, if ever taught in the standardized school systems. Those school systems are instead largely preparing students for entry into the corporate business structures of modern society.

This lack of exposure to a wider range of adaptable skill sets for more professional independence creates another example of "scarcity bias." Due to the belief that professional roles are easily replaceable, many become scared to leave their post to start independent ventures. This results in a greater reliance on corporate institutions for a sense of security around fulfilling personal obligations to the provider role. Rather, we need to learn to embrace an "abundance mindset," characterized by a belief system encouraging resilience, adaptability, and growth.

Professional Roles Break Down The Physical Body— The repetitive movements required in the modern workplace literally break down the physical body. If men are working with their hands, they are pushed into highly-specific roles in assembly lines where each man is completing a small part of the whole product before passing this onto the next step in the assembly line—over and over again.

Before the Industrial Revolution, men practiced skilled crafts where a product was created "from scratch" and molded until final application in a community setting. This involved a much greater range of tasks and required a variety of physical movements. This allowed much less pressure to be put on any one body part all day every day and avoided the repetitive movements associated with "repetitive stress injuries" common in the workplace today.[93] These *repetitive stress injuries* include issues like back injuries and joint/connective tissue problems that won't kill you, but do cause a lot of pain. For many, these injuries will decrease quality of life by the time they hit retirement age. Isn't it ironic to spend one's whole life toiling in labor, only to fall apart in retirement without a chance to even *enjoy* it?

Professional Roles Break Down The Mind— The jobs of modern society *rarely* play a role in contributing to a sense of personal meaning by supporting satisfaction of a worker's core values or personal integrity. Instead, they are usually built around corporate values and missions. In the Old World, each laborer was a craftsman of a skilled trade that was meaningfully passed down through the generations. Not only did a blacksmith learn and practice an interesting and dynamic craft to keep their mind thinking critically to stay sharp into old age, but their last name was *literally* "Smith" to account for the family tradition.

---

93   Downs, D.,G. (1997). Nonspecific work-related upper extremity disorders. *American Family Physician*, 55(4):1296–1302.

This was just another symbol of even greater meaning-making to their daily tasks of productivity. In the modern assembly lines of big business, most employees are cut off from finding a personal sense of integrity in their daily work, let alone feeling intellectually stimulated.

Professional Roles Break Down Relationships—It was not just one or two people working in their skilled trades to provide resources for their family, but a whole community working together. Old World communities were self-sufficient villages that depended on each and every craftsman to complete tasks essential for the community's well-being. This means that when building a carriage, the blacksmith and carpenter worked together closely through the completion of a project. They then watched as their finished product was used to plow a new field that created a tangible sense of personal value in a community setting. This provided community members with very real opportunities to connect meaningfully with each other through sharing their gifts in mutual service to their community. That, in turn, satisfied a personal sense of meaning in everyday life described as "purpose" in this book. Without a shared sense of meaning-making in the professional roles characteristic of everyday life, mere efforts to provide financial resources rarely enable these types of satisfying relationships with others.

Professional Roles Take Away Personal Influence—Businesses in modern society are no longer focused on serving communities or empowering people, but rather on profits for executive boards and stockholders. A business used to serve a community directly and make sure their own mission and values reflected what was required by the community served. While a business sometimes works philanthropy and "giving back" into their corporate mission, these values are rarely created to serve a community, but rather to extract as much value as possible *from* a community member in exchange for a product that maximizes profit for shareholders. Because the purpose of the business is no longer to benefit the community, the meaning behind the work in these roles is often lacking. No longer can we say that we are making a sacrifice for the good of the community, nor can we see the tangible benefits of the work we are doing. Instead, the benefits are generally making the rich richer while we watch our communities crumble.

Losing Faith in Modern Society

Participation in organized religion has dwindled in recent years.[94] In the last ten years, only 65% of Americans report they are "Christians," down by 12% from the previous ten years. More Americans are also reporting a lack of affiliation, with a 9% increase in those identifying as "Atheist or Agnostic." It appears that as our global community continues to progress after the Industrial Revolution, the practical purposes and structure provided by organized religion no longer serve the same adaptive purposes of community structure as once was the case in the isolated farming communities of the Old World. While these practical uses of organized religion might be changing, there are still many adaptive features of healthy spirituality and faith, some of which are addressed in this book.

Romantic Relationships Failing in Modern Society

Earlier we discussed the relatively failed state of romantic relationships in modern society where roughly half of marriages end in divorce and *more* than half of second marriages end in divorce. This can be a scary statistic, so let's take a moment to remember that when it comes to *real romance,* this is still a

94   Pew Research Center, Oct. 17, 2019, "In U.S., Decline of Christianity Continues at Rapid Pace"

relatively new skill set for most people because in most cases, people are still prepared for social life based on traditional gender expectations from the Old World.

Since most of us are only a few generations from an isolated farming community, many people are largely lost when it comes to the rules of engagement and healthy boundaries for a romantic relationship in modern society, where social expectations are much more fluid in a world no longer bound by the structure once required by the Old World. These changing social and economic dynamics have created a need for people to update behaviors and belief systems if they want to build a healthy and balanced romantic relationship that includes passion and lust. In many ways, the traditional gender expectations of the Old World will no longer work.

Here are just a few of the missing skill sets and belief systems required for a meaningful and satisfying relationship in Modern Society:

Conflict resolution skills are essential to navigate tension in a way that solves the issue at hand by incorporating all of the information available to make the most educated decision possible, while also minimizing resentment, promoting cohesion, and increasing understanding/trust between community members through this negotiation process. Men tend to be minimally exposed to the dynamic interpersonal skills required for this type of communication with others because in the Old World, men were allowed "veto power" for most big decisions as part of their traditional role as protector.

Further, men are underprepared for *emotional self-regulation* and *healthy communication* with others due to the traditional expectations for men to block self-awareness, emotional expression, affection, as well as help seeking behavior, as discussed in detail in chapter 3.

Men are also underprepared for *domestic household tasks* and *child-rearing* due to their traditional primary focus being on providing resources by making money outside of the home, rather than skills that involve completing tasks inside the household or involving caretaking. A recent study in 2013 showed that while 80% of men are now involved in their children's lives, only 50% believe they are doing a good job.[95] Research has also shown that for nonresident fathers, a child's well-being is less associated with sharing resources like time or money, and more about being actively involved in *shared meaningful activities*, an area where many men have very few personal experiences with their own fathers in their own childhood for reference.[96]

On the opposite side of traditional manhood belief systems and behavioral expectations, girls and women are often taught the opposite behaviors—such as passivity and reliance on male assertiveness for decision-making, rather than formulating more internally-driven wants, needs and desires. As a result, there is often reinforcement for the social and cultural roles of both men and women that keeps each rigidly confined to their traditional gender expectations.

This results in many romantic relationships getting stuck in a state of "codependency," where each partner struggles to function at an adequate level on their own. Instead of being accountable for their own personal limitations, each redirects blame outward towards their partner or the relationship as the

95   Jones, J., and Mosher, W. D. (2013) Fathers' involvement with their children: United States, 2006 - 2010. National Health Statistics Reports, 71, 2-21. Retrieved from http://www.cdc.gov/nchs/data/nhsr/nhsr071.pdf
96   Adamsons, K., and Johnson, S. K. (2013) An updated and expanded meta-analysis of nonresident fathering and child well-being. *Journal of Family Psychology*, 27(4), 589-599. doi:10.1037/a0033786

cause for their own lack of personal fulfillment. In a relationship that is *not* characterized by *codependency*, each individual can have their own thoughts and feelings independent of the other—even through tension and conflict—while continuing to expect support and security. This is the foundation for an ideal family environment—one where unconditional love, trust, and mutual empowerment is the daily expectation. For the individuals of couples who *do* get caught up in *codependency*, this is stifling for the health and wellness of the *whole* family, but nobody is too far gone to begin developing more self-awareness and communication skills to get different results.

Case Study of Codependency: The Joneses were an upper-class family in a wealthy neighborhood. The father had a high-power executive level job and the mother stopped working once she had children to be a "stay-at-home mom." Father had very little emotional intelligence, but this did not disrupt his ability to be an exceptional provider. Mother had very little ability to advocate for her personal needs, but this did not disrupt her ability to be an attendant mother. They were a good fit administratively, but their different roles came with very different demands and in a relatively short period of time, they grew apart in their marriage. By the time they realized there was a significant problem, the father had become obsessed with work and alcohol, the mother became over-involved with the children, and the children (then teenagers) were symptomatic due to being drawn into this dynamic. As a result, the children were relying on dysfunctional behaviors and belief systems to cope with daily life. Both parents had little faith in their abilities to do the work required to save their relationship and, instead, chose to get a divorce. Interestingly, and perhaps a bit surprisingly, all of the individuals in this family are now both happier and healthier post-divorce than they were as an "intact family."

These urban and industrial developments that are creating a global community have also harmed the natural ecosystems of our planet. With the dramatic increase in population over the last hundred years, human beings are putting more pressure on our natural ecosystem to support its needs than ever before. Between changes in land and water use (urbanization, dams, farming GMOs), resource scarcity (deforestation, water scarcity, wildlife decline), and climate change (increase temperature of land and water, extreme storms, and sea level rise)[97], we are approaching a point where human ingenuity will no longer buffer the negative health outcomes faced by our species if nothing changes.

Most people would agree with the idea that human beings are the most intelligent species on the planet. In fact, we have adapted to our environments so well, that we are actually putting ourselves and our entire ecosystem at risk through our dominance. Now, as a global community, humankind has a great responsibility to extend the power of our dynamic problem solving to a rescue operation on a global scale. Men have always had more political influence relative to their female counterparts. But for men to heal ourselves and play a role in healing this planet, we must use that influence to purposefully loosen the male grip on executive influence and allow women and other marginalized voices to share the responsibility of community leadership. Further, this will require men breaking through the social and cultural expectations of the Old World. The belief systems and behavior expectations from traditional manhood keep males out of touch with their own basic needs and that of their community members. This lack of personal integration represents a significant barrier for men when it

97   Myers SS, Patz J (2009) Emerging threats to human health from global environmental change. *Annual Review of Environmental Resources*, 34:223–252.

comes to protecting personal health and well-being, not to mention fulfilling the sacred roles of protector and provider for an emerging global community.

Whether you choose to invest in the long-term future of our world is one thing, but the health and well-being of men is at high-risk as we speak. There is no waiting for a future generation to make these changes as men are dying younger and with lower quality of life than our female peers. Traditional men are simply unfit to "take the reins" as adaptable providers, protectors, and community leaders in modern society. This is not a future problem. This is a *right now* problem!

When we do not take responsibility for updating our belief systems and behavioral habits, the rigid patterns of traditional manhood result in higher rates of self-neglect, social isolation, addiction and even suicide. One hundred years ago from when this book was written in 1920, life expectancy for women was only two years greater than males and now 100 years later, men die an average of six years younger than women.[98] If there continues to be scientific progress developing new and improved healthcare interventions, then why has the life expectancy of women outpaced men so significantly?

In the early 2000s, public health officials noticed that suicide rates climbed by 30% from 2000 through 2016.[99] While suicide was the 10th leading cause of death in 2016 for the general population, it was the second leading cause of death for young people age 10-34 (second only to accidents) and the fourth leading cause of death for people age 35-54. Of the

---

98   A.M. Minino et al. (2002). "Deaths: Final Data for 2000," *National Vital Statistics Reports* 50, no. 15; Ian P.F. Owens, "Sex Differences in Mortality Rates," *Science*, 297 (September 20, 2002): 2008-2009.

99   Hedegaard, H., et al. (2018). Suicide rates in the United States continue to increase. NCHS Data Brief No. 309. National Center for Health Statistics. Available at ww.cdc.gov/nchs/products/databriefs/db309.htm.

suicide deaths taking place between 2000-2012, males made up 70% of them and 60% of suicides involve cases of depression without adequate treatment.[100]

Why are so many men *not* receiving adequate treatment for their mental health, you might ask? Men are 50% less likely to get diagnosed with "internalizing disorders" like anxiety or depression because males tend to avoid open expression of pain or fear, which makes the sadness one would expect from depression, or the nervousness one would expect from anxiety difficult to see. Instead, men and boys with depression and/or anxiety tend to express irritability, social isolation, sensitivity to threats of perceived respect, compulsivity, physical pain, insomnia, low motivation, and poor concentration.[101]

Men are more likely to be diagnosed with "externalizing disorders" characterized by acting out, addiction, and the anger outbursts associated with a perceived "lack of empathy for others" often characterized by a diagnosis of *Narcissistic Personality Disorder*.[102] Men are not being adequately diagnosed with depression and anxiety because of the social and cultural training that blocks seeking help in the name of independence.

As a result of these social and cultural pressures, men are more likely to get caught up in overidentification with professional accolades, physical power, collecting financial wealth, and even compulsive behavior like addiction or

100   American Foundation of Suicide Prevention (2015). *Facts and figures*. Retrieved from https://www.afsp.org/understanding-suicide/facts-and-figures

101   Martin, L. A., Neighbor, H. W., and Griffith, D. M. (2013). The experience of symptoms of depression in men vs women: Analysis of the National Comorbidity Survey Replication. *JAMA Psychiatry*, 70(10), 1100-1106. doi:10.1001/jamapsychiatry.2013.1985

102   American Psychiatric Association. (2013). *Diagnostic and statistical manual of mental disorders* (5th ed.). https://doi.org/10.1176/appi.books.9780890425596

controlling the behavior of others in personal relationships. All of these are attempts to experience a personal sense of safety and security in daily life.

The more these behaviors and belief systems are reinforced by the social and cultural expectations of traditional manhood that must be used to access male privilege, the more men are likely to overidentify with them. This in turn, sets many men up for problems when they rely on these tactics (including violence) to interact with vulnerable community members who men have been both biologically and socially charged with *protecting*—or at the *least* doing no harm to.

The social and cultural training for males from traditional manhood doesn't always end in suicide or homicide obviously. There is a wide range of negative outcomes for the health and well-being of men that can result from becoming too dependent on the behaviors and belief systems of traditional manhood to feel comfortable in our own skin. In fact, sometimes boys grow into men who *appear* to be well-adjusted in the face of these pressures. You can consider the following range:

1. Well-adjusted man with minimal regrets and high quality of life due to personal meaning found outside of professional roles and surrounded by loved ones in meaningful relationships.

2. Learning to be a passive consumer and settle for a life absent of personal meaning, but while consciously avoiding most of what people would consider "hardship," only to struggle with depression after retirement because so much of self-identity was wrapped up inside of professional roles.[103] This

103   Lee J, Smith JP. Work, retirement, and depression. *Journal of Population Ageing.* 2009; 2: 57–71. 10.1007/s12062-010-9018-0

overidentification with professional roles to maintain the "good provider" status comes with a lot of social and cultural reinforcement, but also leaves men open to a lack of personal meaning after those roles have ended in retirement.

3. Some men will sense that something is off before retirement, but instead of heeding the signs will mistake these symptoms as the natural consequences of getting older and having more responsibilities. In reality, the aches and pains are the first indications of wear and tear that easily develops into chronic health issues if not addressed. These symptoms decrease quality of life and sometimes even contribute to a shorter lifespan.

4. Many men reach midlife to have the dreaded "midlife crisis." This is what psychology refers to as an "existential crisis," where to put it simply, a person's own *existence*—i.e. "self-identity"—comes into question because there has been such an abrupt and significant change that our old belief systems are no longer relevant. This calls into question our own mortality and natural fear of death that is not only normal, but also shared with most other animals.[104] It is the fear itself that keeps a person hyperaware of their own mortality and for many men, this is the first time they have allowed themselves to fully experience this level of uncertainty on a more personal level. This can be a helpful experience as long as this person course corrects towards their authentic self-identity, rather than just "doubling down" on whatever behaviors and belief systems are already available to avoid the fear of

104   Adolphs R. (2013). The biology of fear. *Current biology : CB, 23*(2), R79–R93. https://doi.org/10.1016/j.cub.2012.11.055

their own shadow. This is where the stories of sports cars, infidelity, and nasty divorces comes from.

5. Some men develop symptoms of depression as learned helplessness[105] or symptoms of anxiety as an honest attempt to keep up with and control the high pace and inevitable chaos of the natural world.[106] These are known as "internalizing symptoms" because they are largely experienced internally. There is currently more public acceptance around seeking medical support and treatment of these issues, rather than "externalizing disorders" that men are commonly diagnosed with.

> a. Men are diagnosed with *internalizing disorders* at only 50% the rate of women, but this is believed to be underreported because men are more likely to show anger/irritability in adherence to traditional manhood,[107] rather than nervousness, sadness, and inappropriate guilt—the features mental health professionals are trained to assess for.

6. Some men become obsessed with a form of compulsive self-soothing (escapism) to self-medicate the pain by using alcohol, drugs, or high-risk behavior, like sex, gambling, or controlling others. These

105   Forgeard, M. J., Haigh, E. A., Beck, A. T., Davidson, R. J., Henn, F. A., Maier, S. F., Mayberg, H. S., and Seligman, M. E. (2011). Beyond Depression: Towards a Process-Based Approach to Research, Diagnosis, and Treatment. *Clinical psychology : a publication of the Division of Clinical Psychology of the American Psychological Association*, 18(4), 275–299. https://doi.org/10.1111/j.1468-2850.2011.01259.x

106   Robinson, O. J., Vytal, K., Cornwell, B. R., and Grillon, C. (2013). The impact of anxiety upon cognition: perspectives from human threat of shock studies. *Frontiers in human neuroscience*, 7, 203. https://doi.org/10.3389/fnhum.2013.00203

107   Addis, 2008.

mental health issues are referred to as "externalizing symptoms" because they are largely experienced as "acting out" behavior. With the rise in popularity of calling controlling men "narcissists," it does not appear that we are getting closer to having more public acceptance that this behavior is the reflection of untreated mental health issues, rather than a sole focus on their acting out behavior at the surface.

> a. Men are diagnosed with externalizing disorders at higher rates than women[108] because there is no requirement to express vulnerable emotions. The behavior is all about redirecting the personal discomfort either into addiction or anger-driven behavior that is designed to control other people in order to protect the user from their own perceived vulnerability.

7. Immediate danger to self or others—homicidal or suicidal

Men have inherited a great responsibility from our ancestors to protect our family and community from potential threats with our relative physical power and social influence, but how are we going to be protectors if we cannot take care of ourselves enough to stay healthy and emotionally stable—or even *alive*?

The behavior expectations and belief systems still taught as parts of traditional manhood—that personal success is based on winning in competition against others, asking for help or expressing emotions is a sign of weakness, and a willingness to accept violence as a means to an end as a sign of a good leader—

108   Cochran, S. V., and Rabinowitz, F. E. (2003). Gender-sensitive recommendations for assessment and treatment of depression in men. *Professional Psychology: Research and Practice, 34*(2), 132–140. https://doi. org/10.1037/0735-7028.34.2.132

makes for fierce providers and protectors in the isolated farming communities of the Old World, but what about the concrete jungles of modern society? A healthy and humane sense of personal meaning is nowhere to be found in a man's role as a provider and protector in the modern concrete jungles that are now ruled by corporate conglomerates.

The experiences of boys growing into adulthood are guided by the same social and cultural forces of traditional manhood that block adult men from accessing a full range of emotional intelligence necessary to gain the insight required for creating personal meaning. There are no "bad emotions"—just standard emotional experiences that *all* human beings are designed for on a basic neurological level to guide meaningful connection to our own existence, as well as relationships to other people.

With a limited range of skill development in this area from traditional manhood, men are vastly underprepared to find personal meaning in life. This is because males are literally taught to be scared of the emotional information itself as a sign of lacking worth and value as a "real man." From this perspective, it is easy to see how this social and cultural training still has its place in some circumstances, but when adhered to rigidly actually sets men up for mental health symptoms: a lack of personal meaning and life satisfaction, social isolation, depression/anxiety, domestic violence, and even suicide.

When we see it all together, our situation can be daunting. There appears to be a lot of work to do and from this position, it is all too easy to stay in denial and try to avoid the discomfort of the unknown. But before you stick your head back in the sand, are you ready for the good news?

The same missing elements that are necessary for men to heal ourselves—a full range of emotional intelligence, greater personal meaning in life based on our own unique humanity and interpersonal skills focused on collaboration rather than coercion—are actually the *same* missing pieces that are required to fulfill the sacred role of warrior/protector and hunter/ provider in our newly emerging global community. Men must be willing to tolerate different ideas and people—even actively make a place for them at the table—if we are to serve a much more diverse global community.

This concept of leadership as an ideal position for service work was proposed in the 1970s with the philosophical work of Robert Greenleaf[109] as an explanation for why community members have lost trust in the institutions of modern society. Greenleaf's concepts were championed by the Evangelical Christian community, who recognized the similarity between this process and the story of Jesus Christ. Since then, this concept known as "servant leadership" has enjoyed a wide range of use in the professional world, where successful business leaders and entrepreneurs seem to understand the adaptability of this mindset to develop healthy and high-functioning systems of relationships for group success. There are indeed many applications in business leadership, but what if we make the context even *more* broad to include our emerging global community as another system of relationships?

To make the significant changes required for personal and leadership development, a person must force themselves outside of the comfort zone that reinforces old habits. This requires an active and deliberate choice made on a regular basis to push into the relative discomfort of change. Otherwise, people remain stuck with the passive choice to remain the same, even if we *want* there to be different results.

---

109   Greenleaf, R. K. (1977). Servant leadership: A journey into the nature of legitimate power and greatness. Paulist Press.

As human beings, we are fundamentally social animals because these skills have always provided an evolutionary advantage. What better way to enhance a process of personal development for human beings than in the context of our relationships? I might be a bit biased as a licensed marriage and family therapist who personally fell in love with the field for this very reason, but the evidence from my own life experiences and the evidence-based research is clear—there is no better way to get realistic and sustainable results when it comes to the personal development and overall health of human beings.

This departure from the old familiar world first requires a person to realize something is "off," then have enough willingness to answer this call to leave the familiarity of the comfort zone behind and enter the great unknown. It is only within this unfamiliar landscape where someone has an opportunity to face new trials and tribulations unlike anything ever experienced before, and through them, to develop gifts that had not yet had a chance to emerge. Once these missing pieces are attained, the journeyer is able to return home from the unfamiliar world with the knowledge required to serve their community meaningfully in a mutually empowering position with these newfound gifts.

This experience has been referred to as "The Hero's Journey"[110] by the great comparative mythologist Joseph Campbell. The character arc has been used extensively and can be seen in the journeys of growth towards personal meaning of both Jesus Christ and Siddhartha (before becoming known as "Buddha"). Modern storytelling has used the Hero's Journey for characters such as Neo in the Matrix and Luke Skywalker in Star Wars.

---

110   Campbell, J. (2004). The hero with a thousand faces. Princeton, N.J: Princeton University Press.

It is only through this type of sacred journey—one that is bigger than our own individual existence—that we can leave our familiar world behind to go through the tests necessary to find and then polish our gifts so that we may share them with the world. It is these experiences inside of a meaningful process of change and growth that force people to leave the familiar thoughts, feelings, behavior, and belief systems behind to stimulate our *true* destiny that lies dormant in the shadows of what we consciously understand as self-identity.

If you are reading this book right now, then you are well on your way. Regardless of what you decide to do—or not to do—after learning this information, it has been an honor to be a small part of your journey up to this point.

CHAPTER 6: BOYS ARE HUMAN BEINGS TOO

The last chapter showed the connections between men's mental health and *gender role conflict* that comes as a direct result of accessing *male privilege* according to the rules of traditional manhood in modern society. This process begins with indoctrination that starts in childhood.

In childhood, boys are taught that a "real man" is emotionally-restricted, hyperfocused on achievement as a sign of "success," feels no pain or fear, and is willing to take high risks and/or use violence to achieve those means. As boys enter adulthood, the social pressure for conforming to these expectations will reach its peak, but the early signs are evident in statistics around kids going to their doctor.

It is estimated that 1 in 3 kids will experience anxiety symptoms, but boys only make up 30% of anxiety diagnoses in pediatric healthcare settings, versus 70% of girls. Girls age 14-25 are also twice as likely to be diagnosed with depression.[111] As discussed earlier, boys tend not to report the *internalizing symptoms* characteristic of anxiety and depression, so their cases are missed altogether until they begin to act out with *externalizing symptoms* like the problematic behavior associated with Attention Deficit Hyperactivity Disorder (ADHD), Oppositional Defiant Disorder (ODD), substance abuse or Conduct Disorder.[112] Many times these cases for boys are missed altogether—mistaken as an example of "boys being boys."

111   Cochran, S. V., and Rabinowitz, F. E. (2003). Gender-sensitive recommendations for assessment and treatment of depression in men. Professional Psychology, 34(2), 132–140. doi:10.1037/0735-7028.34.2.132
112   Lynch, J., and Kilmartin, C. (2013). The pain behind the mask: Overcoming masculine depression (2nd ed.). New York, NY: Routledge

Boys and men are two to three times more likely to be diagnosed with *externalizing disorders* like ADHD, ODD, Narcissism, and addiction.[113] Not only are boys flying under the radar with their mental and emotional health, but they are also less likely to report their experience of abuse. Again, this requires acknowledging their experience of being dominated, which boys are taught is a sign of "weakness" and likeness to "femininity." Boys are four to fourteen times less likely to disclose sexual assault,[114] even though it is estimated that roughly one in six boys will be sexually assaulted.[115]

The problem here is *not* that men and boys are blood-thirsty animals incapable of managing violent impulses. Rather the behaviors and belief systems taught to boys create men who are proficient problem solvers and warriors on good days, but who lack important elements necessary to cope with stress in a way that is compatible with our modern society—like resilience in the face of adversity, poor self-awareness, and emotional regulation, as well as limited social skills and even a habit for isolation at the times our humanity is programmed to rely on the safety of our loved ones the most.

When there is enough tension between the demands of the environment and our ability to meet those demands, men are prone to separating themselves from their own humanity or dehumanizing others to a point of limiting the basic needs and

---

113   Kiselica, M. S., Englar-Carlson, M., and Horne, A. M. (Eds.) (2008). Counseling troubled boys: A guidebook for professionals. New York, NY: Routledge

114   Holmes, G.R., Offen, L., and Waller, G. (1997). See no evil, hear no evil, speak no evil: Why do relatively few male victims of childhood sexual abuse receive help for abuse-related issues in adulthood? *Clinical Psychology Review*, 17, 69-88.

115   Finkelhor, D., Hotaling, G., Lewis, I. A., and Smith, C. (1990). Sexual abuse in a national survey of adult men and women: Prevalence, characteristics, and risk factors. *Child Abuse and Neglect*, 14, 19-28. doi:10.1016/0145-2134(90)90077-7

rights of themselves and those around them—even resulting in unthinkable violence like suicide and mass murder.

If men report emotional pain, fear, or lack of motivation, they are socially viewed as "weak, stupid or lazy." Without adequate skills of self-regulation and communication, this type of interaction often ends in more tension with social ties, which only limits access to social resources and commonly results in symptoms only getting worse. Since there are limited options for self-expression to cope with emotional discomfort as biologically programmed, boys and men who struggle with anxiety and/or depression symptoms are more likely to express irritability and behavior/control issues, rather than express chronic sadness, nervousness, or lack of personal life satisfaction.

While the social policing from caregivers, authority figures and peers is not helpful for supporting the health of young people, it *does* tend to form the basis for how they learn to relate to themselves. Kids can be heard speaking to themselves out loud in a natural process of human learning called "external processing" in developmental psychology. They then later *internalize* this process as they get older and social demands get more complex.[116]

By the time someone reaches adulthood, they have usually internalized this *self-talk* so you will no longer hear it out loud under normal circumstances. However, this narration of personal experience can still be heard spoken out loud by adults during times of stress. There is an old saying in behavioral science that, "in times of *stress*, we *regress*." In fact, people can oftentimes be heard narrating hardship *out loud*. If you listen closely, you can hear people reinforcing an unhealthy image

---

116   Crick, N. R., and Dodge, K. A. (1994). A review and reformulation of social information-processing mechanisms in children's social adjustment. *Psychological Bulletin, 115,* 74–101.

of themselves during times of stress. You might have heard a person doing this when they look confused at the grocery store, obviously unsure about the final items on their list that was left at home and muttering to themselves something like, "do we have cereal? I'm not sure...How could you forget the list *again*? So *stupid*..."

Whether you are consciously aware of the internal self-talk that narrates the thoughts in your head, everyone has their own brand. Oftentimes, the social policing we received in childhood plays a significant role in how we learn to do that. Social policing and criticism is internalized as a personal defense against potential social rejection. In the process of learning these habits to avoid social rejection, the natural parts of self that are the focus of social policing are labeled "NOT ACCEPTABLE" by our personal identity and pushed down into unconscious awareness as a form of self-preservation as a social being.

This type of self-talk is one of many different "defense mechanisms" we learn as a child to secure and protect our basic needs. Since the natural world is chaotic and children already have limited control at the mercy of their caretakers, a collection of *defense mechanisms* are unconsciously created to stay safe from real or perceived threats in the outside world. These include obvious threats to physical safety, but also include the social policing efforts from family, caretakers, and peer groups that represent a risk of social rejection. A collection of preferred *defense mechanisms* keeps people safe in a familiar "comfort zone" of emotional and cognitive awareness—also called "ego" by Sigmund Freud.[117]

---

117   Freud, S. (1961). The ego and the id. In J. Strachey (Ed. and Trans.), *The standard edition of the complete psychological works of Sigmund Freud* (Vol. 19, pp. 3-66). London: Hogarth Press.

Case study: Joe was a successful business owner who seemed to have it all together on the outside - the family, large home, luxury vehicles, and a financial pace that would allow an early retirement. He overcame a lot of obstacles growing up at home with an absent father and a mother with untreated psychiatric issues. As a boy, Joe responded to his mother's worsening mental health with his own attempts to bring up her spirit through his ongoing playful engagement towards her. Joe was also intelligent and did well in school, then quickly became a talented salesman as an adult because he was already so familiar with "turning it on" in a playful yet patient way as a child with his mother. This made his clients very fond of him and combined with his intelligence, his business became very successful relatively quickly. While Joe was exceptional at making money and retaining clients, he had very little trust for people outside of these controlled transactions. As a result, his marriage was failing, he had no close friends, and was not involved in his broader community.

Many boys start practicing these *defense mechanisms* that protect the *ego* at a *very* young age, since they have always been a part of self-preservation. For most men and boys, the defenses available from the belief systems and behavioral expectations of traditional manhood are readily available and come with limited risk of immediate social rejection. These strategies tend to be very effective in the moment—even helping a user of *male privilege* feel powerful and in control through tension and conflict—but again at the cost of personal authenticity and cohesion in important relationships. This almost inevitably results in social isolation and the neglect of basic needs.

The social nature of human beings only serves to continue reinforcing a reliance on these belief systems and behavior expectations through the lifespan. Since people tend to associate with other "like-minded" individuals ("birds of feather flock *together*"), boys and men who more actively participate in upholding the standards of traditional manhood commonly seek out like-minded friends who also more actively participate in social policing. This creates a self-reinforcing culture where those belief systems and behavior expectations become more commonplace within that social setting. Unless men make the conscious and personally uncomfortable choice to get outside of the comfort zones offered by male privilege and reinforced through social policing, the outlook for life satisfaction, meaningful relationships, and optimal health and well-being is grim.

The more a man benefits from the male privilege offered by institutions of social influence, the more likely men are to be confined by the pressure to maintain those resulting behaviors and belief systems.[118] It is easy to assume that the existence of male privilege itself is a sign that men must benefit from its use but in reality, the more men rigidly cling to these behaviors and belief systems, the more restricted and less adaptable men become.[119]

It is important to remember that social influence in and of itself is *not* a "bad thing." As stated in the movie *Forrest Gump* by the main character's mother, "stupid is as stupid does."[120] Momma Gump was imparting this wisdom of resilience onto her son that you cannot judge a tool by its appearance, but only

118   Mankowski, E. S., and Maton, K. I. (2010). A community psychology of men and masculinity: Historical and conceptual review. *American Journal of Community Psychology*, 45(1-2), 73–86. doi:10.1007/s10464-009-9288-y

119   Liu, W. M., and Ali, S. R. (2005). Addressing social class and classism in vocational theory and practice: Extending the emancipatory communitarian approach. *The Counseling Psychologist*, 33(2), 189–196. doi:10.1177/0011000004272269

120   Zemeckis, R. (1994). *Forrest Gump*. Paramount Pictures.

on how it is used—and as we are reminded by the character of Forrest Gump, a low level of intellect can be quite adaptive if used with high integrity! Would it not be safe to assume that *intelligence* also "is as it does," or that any other type of strength or asset is as it *does*?

The social influence available through accessing male privilege—however attractive in the moment that it might be—is usually a barrier to personal growth, fulfillment, and the health and safety of men and their fellow community members.

These oftentimes invisible forces come from many different directions to reinforce these constraints on men and boys. There is the immediate *social pressure* to fit in and be accepted and environmental pressure to fulfill traditional roles ffor providing resources to and protecting loved ones. Men also face pressure from their own worldview to stay in their familiar comfort zone defined by use of the defense mechanisms available from traditional manhood to seek mastery within their immediate environment. When and if males do step outside of traditional manhood in an attempt to honor their full humanity, then they can rightfully expect to have less access to resources as a direct result.

Thus the trappings of traditional manhood keep men and boys from adapting resiliently along with our changing environments, which is now a part of daily life in a fast-paced and highly-connected modern society. Personal experiences beyond our familiar world are *required* to develop confidence, authentic self-identity, and self-esteem. But most men actually have *less* room to put this into practice in adulthood as a direct result of overreliance on male privilege. This perverts a concept of self as an adaptive human being, where personal identity only gets smaller and more restricted over time for most men as they get trapped inside of the foxholes of male privilege, originally dug out to provide safety, security and even a competitive edge.

Many men are surprised when they realize "building self-esteem" involves formation of a self-identity beyond the markers of traditional manhood (*strength, independence, achievement,* etc.) because to their existing worldview, this tends to sound counterintuitive. Sometimes personal awareness of the needed changes only happens after a crisis—such as a midlife crisis, the first jolts of personal health issues, or the death of a friend—because it takes that much pressure on the old and ingrained habits of one's comfort zone to create enough critical awareness outside of an existing worldview.

The more we know who we are—and who we are *not*—it becomes much easier to intentionally manage our personal thoughts, feelings, behaviors, and belief systems to remain in line with authentic self-identity and our most important relationships. In turn, this provides an opportunity to create space for abundance and joy in daily life that meets our basic needs to mutually support ourselves and our loved ones as we meaningfully "hunt as a pack"—as designed by our DNA.

Nobody is solely defined by their social status and *anybody* who tries to pretend that they are will fall flat, because social status has no real value without a stable sense of self-identity to support health promoting behaviors and high quality of life. This stable sense of self-identity is often tricky for people today in modern society because people are usually so far removed from their cultures of origin and natural ecosystems. There cannot be a stable self-identity when the foundation is built on sand!

The tricky part comes in when we fast forward to modern society, where very few people still have access to this cultural wisdom from their ancestors. Most people have been entirely displaced and disconnected from their nation of origin. Further, they have bowed to social pressure to conform to the dominant cultural expectations for accessing available resources. To access these resources, people often must give up their own unique genesis story. The first step to identifying authentic self-identity for people today, is first stripping away the pieces that we are *not*—which as you can see is usually more than people assume at the outset of this process.

Stripping away our false self-identity is a *lot* easier said than done. In Chapter 3, we discussed how our social worldview is *central* to how we experience the world as human beings. This makes disruption of this worldview feel very uncomfortable and often triggers what Freud called an *existential crisis* or what Kübler-Ross outlined in the *phases of grief.*

This is where all of those lessons from a boy's childhood blocks most men from identifying an authentic self-identity as a human being. Instead, many men hunker down in a foxhole of leverage through social influence and convince themselves that if they just grit their teeth silently through the pain long enough, they can "pull themselves up by the bootstraps." As a result, it is all too easy for many men to rely on false—even harmful narratives of self-identity from traditional manhood to create a buffer against unconscious insecurities.

Because this access represents a "lifeline" for retaining social position, many men face a sense of desperation to maintain their social leverage against this perceived assault at all costs. In many ways it is very similar to the process of addiction, where the user continues their compulsive behavior to self-medicate personal discomfort and remain in denial of pain that would surely come to the surface (at least temporarily) if they accepted that their behavior had indeed become problematic.

It is all but impossible to stay healthy and stable as a man, provider, protector, husband, and productive member of society unless basic human needs can be met and honored. But before meeting those human needs is possible, a person must navigate their own grieving process to consciously separate the barriers of traditional manhood from an authentic sense of self-identity as human beings.

This lack of integration is where most men reside today. This often leads to loss of trust in self or others, instability in one's personal life and relationships, and a loss of trust required for a healthy and adaptive community lifestyle. With this said, it is also possible to use human social programming to heal these unresolved wounds, and to ultimately help us fulfill our social obligations to serve and protect an emerging global community in the same ways that Jesus Christ spoke about as "acts of service" and Buddha spoke of as "dharma." However this first requires an integration of a person's full humanity back into self-identity.

Let's take a look at your self-identity at this point.

Self-Identity Exercises:

These exercises are designed to support the reader in exploring and reinforcing a *healthy* and *realistic* **self-identity**. After learning about the general expectations for men in modern society, it is now time to consider the *unique* **Family Culture and Social History** that mixed with those general expectations to influence your own unique self-identity today.

1. What country or region did your Family live in before they came to the United States? _____

    a.   Were Family Members accepted into the social class known as "white?" **[YES or NO]**

    b.   If "NO," what was/is the ethnic and/or racial identity? How were they treated upon arrival to their current country of residence?

_____

_____

_____

_____

2. How much money and/or access to resources did Family already have with them upon arrival? *16% of native-born citizens live below the poverty line, while 20% of immigrants live in poverty.*

_____

_____

_____

_____

3. Did family ancestors come to this country by their own free will? Or to escape the risk of harm by war, famine, or captured and transported for human trafficking (including "slavery"). Write a few sentences that capture the "migration story" of your ancestors. If your ancestors are Native American Indians, please capture this story as one of "forced migration":

_____

_____

_____

_____

Traditional manhood markers: *Success Through Winning (in competition); Emotional Restriction; Strength and Courage; Independence; Acceptance of Violence*

1.   Access to financial resources and social influence as a marker of "success" and/or "winning"

    a. What stands out for you when considering *your* unique family culture and having financial resources and the ability to influence the behavior of other people?

_____

_____

    b. Have you inherited—or plan to inherit—money or influence from Family? **[YES or NO]**

        i.   Includes monetary gifts, financial help with bills, and/or trips

_____

    c. If "YES," what are your obligations (implied or literal) to keep your access to those financial resources and/or social influence? Could the resources and/or support of loved ones (including Love and Belonging) be withdrawn if you fail to meet those obligations? How so?

_____

_____

    d. If "NO," what have you learned to secure access to financial resources and/or social influence on your own?

_____

_____

How did these experiences of your ancestor's shape your self-identity today? What are parts of Self that create *gender role conflict* for "being successful" both inside AND outside the home? What are natural parts of Self that **CANNOT** change? What are parts of Self you would like to *develop*?

_____

_____

_____

2.   *Emotional Restriction* (Anger is allowed and sometimes "happy," but *not* "too much")

What stands out for you when considering *your* unique family culture and having access to a full range of emotions BEYOND anger (and maybe a *little* "happy")

_____

_____

_____

a. Did you see a male parent and/or caregiver expressing a FULL range of Emotions? How did this impact their level of respect given by loved ones? [**YES or NO**]

_____

_____

_____

b. If "NO," what are your obligations (implied or literal) regarding emotions in order to keep a desired level of respect with self and/or loved ones? How would respect be taken away from self and/or loved ones if you *DID* show a full range of emotion?

_____

_____

_____

c. If "YES," how have you learned to manage those emotions in the community at large outside of home and family life?

_____

_____

_____

How have these experiences and observations shaped your own self-identity? What are parts of Self that create *gender role conflict* for being seen as a "real man" both inside AND outside the home? What are natural parts of Self that cannot change? What are parts of Self you would like to *develop*?

_____

_____

_____

_____

3.   *Strength and Courage* (shown by absence of fear, insecurity, and/or pain)

> a.   What stands out for you when considering *your* unique family culture and being able to openly seek safety/acceptance from loved ones when expressing *fear, insecurity*, and/or *pain*?
>
> _____
> _____
> _____
>
> b.   Where did you go when you were scared or hurt as a child? How did caretakers respond? Did they give you space to experience your emotions with supportive and unconditional Love? [**YES or NO**]
>
> c.   If "NO," what are your obligations (implied or literal) with keeping pain/fear to Self when it comes to having the desired level of respect with self and/or loved ones? How would this be disrupted with self and/or loved ones if you *DID* openly show fear/pain?
>
> _____
> _____
> _____
>
> d.   If "YES," how have you learned to manage those emotions in the community at large outside of the Home and Family?
>
> _____
> _____
> _____

How have these experiences shaped self-identity? What are parts of Self that create *gender role conflict* for "being a strong man" both inside *and* outside the home? What are natural parts of Self that *cannot* change? What are parts of Self you would like to *develop*?

_____
_____
_____
_____

4.   *Independence*—A preference to complete tasks individually, rather than depending on the reliability of others or asking for help.

   a.   What stands out for you when considering *your* unique family culture and being able to ask for help? Versus the pressure to "handle it on your own"?

   _____
   _____
   _____

   b.   Who did you ask for help growing up? How did they respond? Did they provide space to support your learning—or NOT? **[YES or NO]**

   _____
   _____
   _____

   c.   If "NO," how would they tell you that tasks must be completed independently? Verbally or nonverbally? How would your level of respect be impacted in the home if you completed those tasks on your own? And what would happen if you did *not* figure out how to complete those tasks on your own?

   _____
   _____
   _____

   d.   If "YES," how have you learned to manage working closely with other people and/or asking for help in the community at large outside of the home and family?

   _____
   _____
   _____

   How have these experiences with independence shaped self-identity? What are parts of self that create *gender role conflict* for "being an independent man" both inside AND outside the home? What are natural parts of self that **CANNOT** change? What are parts of self you would like to *develop*?

   _____
   _____
   _____
   _____

5.   *Acceptance of Violence*—If violence is required to "get a situation under control," then a man must be willing to use violence in order to "get the job done."

> a. What stands out for you when considering *your* unique family culture and being willing to engage in violent behavior in order to "get the job done?"

> _____

> _____

> b. Was there physical violence in the home? Maybe other unfair tactics of *Power and Control* that do not involve *physical aggression,* but still involve coercion and manipulative behavior?— **[YES or NO]**

> _____

> _____

> c. If "YES," what were *your* experiences with *violence* and/or the unfair use of social influence to control the behavior of other people? What did you observe? What happened to you? What have you done towards other people?

> _____

> _____

> d. If "NO," how have you learned to manage conflict with other people and/or set appropriate limits with others in the home? And in the community at large outside of the home and family? Are they similar or different to what you experienced growing up? How so?

> _____

> _____

How have these experiences with aggression and/or power and control tactics shaped your self-identity? What are parts of self that create *gender role conflict* for "being a real man" in terms of willingness to engage in use of power and/or control tactics both inside AND outside the home? What are natural parts of self that **CANNOT** change? What are parts of self you would *like* to develop, even if you are not confident it can happen completely?

_____

_____

_____

_____

CHAPTER 7: FAITH AS A GUIDE TO HEALTHY CONNECTION & COMMUNITY

"The best way to find yourself is to lose yourself in service to others."—Dalai Lama

Many people have been taught that faith-based practices and spirituality cannot coexist with a belief in science. This sets people up to be "turned off" of one or the other based on the social and cultural belief systems that many people carry from past experiences with different social groups.

The fact of the matter is that there is *no* "right way" or "wrong way" to go about a healthy practice of faith and spirituality as long as you are serving your community while also avoiding harm done towards anyone else. This practice of living in a way that "does no harm" and "provides service to our community" is shared by the teachings of both Jesus Christ and Buddha alike.

The history of faith-based practices is a long and interesting one complete with a lot of political confusion that has created many myths that still exist today. Let's take a moment to understand the role of faith and spirituality in human history and debunk these myths, then we will use the universal truths leftover to help the reader understand how the process of self-healing and saving the world mutually support each other.

Spirituality has been a part of humanity for as long as we have written records from 7,000 years ago.[121] Before then, we

121   Nongbri, Brent (2013). *Before Religion: A History of a Modern Concept.* Yale University Press. ISBN 978-0300154160.

have evidence from grave sites that show early humans buried their dead with nonessential items that suggest a belief in the afterlife.[122] Once community leaders realized that religion could be used to organize and influence the members of a community towards a preferred belief system and behavior expectations, more and more political influence has bled into what we now understand as "organized religion." For this reason, we will only use the word "religion" to describe ideas that are a part of an officially recognized "organized religion," rather than more general faith-based and spiritual practices that have been a part of healthy human communities from the start.

Faith-based practices began through oral traditions. Oral tradition became incredibly important early on in human history for the survival of the nomadic hunter/gatherer communities, as well as the isolated farming communities that defined human civilization from hundreds of thousands of years ago. These communities used stories to provide a valuable framework for capturing essential information required for social cohesion, as well as passing on other basic survival skills to the next generation that would have been impossible without a method of retaining intergenerational knowledge.

Since our early days described here, humans have always relied on a meaningful connection to our community for our species to survive and flourish, and ultimately to rise to our current level of global influence. The structure for communal life offered by organized religion provided another layer of reliability and security for these community expectations.

History of the conflict between science and religion goes back many centuries, but really came to the forefront during

---

122   Harari, Yuval N. author. (2015). *Sapiens: a brief history of humankind.* New York: Harper.

"The Enlightenment" in 1700s Europe. This was a movement centered in Western Europe (France, Britain, Germany) that created *huge* changes in the way people understood laws of the natural world by using the "scientific method."

The *scientific method* introduced a system for understanding the natural world with greater reliability than ever imagined before. This meant that someone could have the personal freedom to think critically on their own, as well as have a requirement to "prove validity" before an idea can be known as "true."[123] This was a *big* change that moved human systems of understanding towards individual and critical thought, rather than an acceptance of tradition as the only organizing force of thought.

The introduction of the scientific method also introduced a political battle over community influence between this new field of knowledge and the established religious institutions that previously held exclusive influence in those isolated farming communities for thousands of years. Before this time, the royal families had executive power and whatever religion that leader and their family followed was given preferred social status and political influence.

This resulted in little to no accountability for royal families and a lack of supervision for religious institutions and leaders, who were given a great deal of influence by the royal family in power. A common outcome was the ability of those in power to control the belief systems, emotional experiences, and resulting behavior of its community members. Given this long history of unchecked influence, there were many abuses of power within

---

123   Dupré, Louis. (2004). *The Enlightenment and the Intellectual Foundations of Modern Culture*, New Haven: Yale University Press.

organized religion and to this day, many people are still the victims of "spiritual abuse."[124]

As you can see, there has been a great deal of political pressure forcing organized religion and science against each other through the years in a way that has resulted in mounting tension between them. Many people hold the incorrect assumption that this must mean science and religion themselves are incompatible, as well as each religion with each other—then are *usually* surprised when they realize how similar the core values and beliefs actually are! Let's take this a bit further with a quick review of these similarities between the most widely practiced faith-based value systems through the world.

All religions of the world, as well as science, have a primary focus on the connections between us, other people, and the forces of the natural world.

Christianity calls this connecting force "God's (unconditional) love" for a human race who is naturally imperfect, but faith in *God's unconditional love* and Jesus Christ "dying for the sins" of human imperfection is a model for having this same unconditional love and faith in ourselves—even when we feel flawed and not good enough at times. This concept of "God is love" is also present in the text of the Bible. The following passage is from John 4:7-12:[125]

"Beloved, let us love one another, because love is from God; everyone who loves is born of God and knows God. Whoever does not love does not know God, for God is love. God's love was revealed among us in this way: God sent his only Son into the world so that we might live through him. In this is love, not

124   Ward, D. J. (2011). The lived experience of spiritual abuse, *Mental Health, Religion and Culture*, 14(9), 899-915, DOI: 10.1080/13674676.2010.536206
125   *English Standard Version Bible*. (2001). John 4:7-12.

that we loved God but that he loved us and sent his Son to be the atoning sacrifice for our sins. Beloved, since God loved us so much, we also ought to love one another. No one has ever seen God; if we love one another, God lives in us, and his love is perfected in us."

Catholicism refers to "The Trinity" as the means of connection between God, Jesus Christ, and a piece of God inside of each person called "The Holy Ghost." The story goes that towards the end of his ministry, Jesus promised that God would send another divine entity known as "the Holy Spirit" in his place to continue his work and that after the resurrection, Jesus shared the doctrine in explicit terms. This came in the forms of Matthew 28:18 to, "go and teach all nations, baptizing them in the name of the Father, and of the Son, and of the Holy Ghost."[126] Followers of Catholicism believe that *the father* and *the son* (Jesus) are distinct entities from the *Holy Ghost*, the latter remaining inside of their followers to guide divine purpose and faith-based behavior.

Hinduism speaks of "Karma" as the driving force of the natural world for each individual person, where choices made now will impact how much things "come your way" in the future. This happens both directly and indirectly, where the energy of our thoughts, feelings, and actions towards others comes back to us directly and immediately in each moment, but also indirectly by way of other people's behavior that has been guided by our influence.[127] In summary, this means that if we do good things, we should expect good things to happen to us, and vice versa.

Buddhism serves as a guide based on the teachings of Buddha around observance of the "Four Noble Truths" to

126   *English Standard Version Bible*. (2001). Matthew 28:18.
127   Brodd, J. (2003). *World Religions*. Winona, MN: Saint Mary's Press. ISBN 978-0-88489-725-5.

escape everyday suffering. These *four truths* are centered around concepts of acceptance of reality as it is, avoidance of craving and desire for external pleasure, as well as "nonattachment" to a concept of self as a fixed and constant being.[128] This allows the release of personal discomfort that results from holding on too tightly to an unpredictable and chaotic natural world that is inherently outside of human control. When people learn to accept life as it is in each moment by maintaining a "mindful state," they will have reached "Enlightenment" and achieve a state of "Nirvana." In this state of *Nirvana*, people are no longer reactive or defensive because they can be flexible with life's ebbs and flows in a state of *nonattachment*, allowing practitioners to remain open to life as it is and as a result, limiting a need for power grabs and coercion that easily infects human communities.

Regardless of the specific organized religion, all of them are guided at the foundation by what is commonly recognized today as "The Golden Rule," where people should treat other people the way they want to be treated. This dynamic extends into the social interactions of our community until it comes back to us with the way we would like to be treated.

Not surprisingly, similar themes are found in the scientific study of the mind and human behavior in psychology and social sciences. Sigmund Freud, the originator of talk therapy, worked with and wrote about the use of "defense mechanisms" by people to stay in a personal state of "denial" regarding their experience of pain and fear of the unknown. Many of these defense mechanisms have stood the test of scientific rigor and hold true in the modern practice of talk therapy. Most notable of them is one that Freud called "Projection."

---

128   Donner, Susan E. (April 2010). "Self or No Self: Views from Self Psychology and Buddhism in a Postmodern Context." *Smith College Studies in Social Work.* 80 (2): 215–227. doi:10.1080/00377317.2010.486361

Projection is the avoidance of personal discomfort by redirecting—or "displacing"—a personal reaction onto someone else so that the host can remain in a more comfortable short-term state of denial. This was and still is a primary focus in a type of talk therapy that Freud used called "psychotherapy," where the therapist provides a safe holding space inside of the working relationship for a client to consciously experience these *projections* as a phenomenon of their *own* unconscious reality, then deal with those unmet needs more consciously with the therapist and as a result, resolve them. Until they are resolved, people often remain locked in their own unconscious self-fulfilling prophecy, where they treat people in a way that strengthens their worst fears and insecurities. This only serves to drive them further into their maladaptive defense mechanisms and towards greater mental instability, rather than healing through healthy relationships with other people.

The idea that a belief in only science means that there is an "absence of faith" is another myth that has been an unfortunate result of the political encroachment on spirituality described earlier. There are two main terms used to describe these belief systems—"agnostic" and "atheist." An agnostic is someone who believes that God is unknowable and can only believe what they can experience directly. An atheist, on the other hand, is a person who completely lacks belief in the existence of God(s).[129] As a result of the historical political tension between institutions of science and religion in the Old World, a personal identification as *agnostic* or *atheist* commonly comes with less social influence,

---

129   Merriam-Webster (n.d.). Citation. In *Merriam-Webster.com dictionary*. Retrieved March 15, 2021, from https://www.merriam-webster.com/dictionary/

an assumption of antisocial intentions and even exclusion in many social and cultural groups today.[130] [131]

If we take a step back from the intergenerational lessons of our cultural ancestors and consider the definition of atheist and agnostic, each of these belief systems includes acknowledgement of the connection between beings who live in the same natural ecosystem participating in and interdependent on the same system of energy/resources. Is this not still "having faith" regarding a belief of interconnectedness between ourselves, other beings, and the natural world in said ecosystem? In fact, there is a growing field of counseling psychology referred to as "Ecopsychology" that employs these very systems of knowledge to support healing and recovery from mental health symptoms.[132]

If we reconsider these old myths upheld by political agendas of the Old World, we can see clearly that human life in general could and would be a *lot* more sustainable if more people were allowed to understand how our physical existence is inherently interconnected with and interdependent on accountability for reciprocity with our own natural ecosystems as human beings.

A loving and nonjudgmental connection between self, other people, and the natural world is the foundation for all spiritual and faith-based practices, as well as approaches from social sciences to heal emotional and psychological pain. Both schools of thought not only promote a similar process of emotional and psychological healing, but they are associated with a similar

130   Gervais, W., Xygalatas, D., McKay, R. *et al.* (2017). Global evidence of extreme intuitive moral prejudice against atheists. *Natural Human Behavior, 1*(0151). https://doi.org/10.1038/s41562-017-0151
131   Atkinson, Q. D. and Bourrat, P. (2011). Beliefs about God, the afterlife and morality support the role of supernatural policing in human cooperation. *Evolution and Human Behavior, 32*, 41–49.
132   Summers, J. K., and Vivian, D. N. (2018). Ecotherapy - A Forgotten Ecosystem Service: A Review. *Frontiers in psychology, 9*, 1389. https://doi.org/10.3389/fpsyg.2018.01389

cascade of physical benefits associated with stimulation of the parasympathetic nervous system. Those benefits promote optimal use of the body's natural healing systems for recovery from immediate stressors, while also increasing lifespan in the long run.

On a more personal and individual level, a secure and emotionally attuned social space (sometimes with a professional counselor or therapist) becomes an opportunity to grow and develop as a human being through participating in what the research calls "corrective emotional experiences." This is where a person becomes stressed out enough in the moment that the sympathetic nervous system fires up for survival with a strong drive to engage in old defense mechanisms focused on self-preservation. However, instead of shutting down or acting out according to those old scripts to recreate old wounds and reinforce limiting belief systems, the safety and attunement of a secure relationship helps guide a person under stress to more safely experience their uncomfortable thoughts and feelings with someone who can be trusted.

When this trusted person hears the emotional pain underneath of the stress and is able to respond in a way that honors the personal discomfort, this shared experience of understanding and acceptance in a time of stress stimulates "mutual soothing" of the parasympathetic nervous system of *both* individuals—allowing the body to regulate its physical stress response while the mind can stay *nonattached* with cognitive and emotional flexibility. Mutual soothing thus provides community members with a safe space to break through old belief systems and habits of behavior that keep everyone stuck in the status quo, especially during times of stress where it is most likely to go back to old defense mechanisms. Even beyond the body's health and the mind's balance, these social skills are also essential for reinforcing reliable connections with others based on mutual respect and support of shared goals. It is that much easier to maintain trust with community members to keep everyone safe and community cohesion high for the ongoing and sustainable support of optimal health and happiness for all members.

There are many different organized religions throughout the world and while each have been popular vehicles for concepts of faith and spirituality to be taught to their followers, modern society has become *much* more connected than the isolated farming communities of the Old World. This has left most religious groups with the leftover residue of political agendas from the ruling elites of the isolated farming communities of the Old World, where these belief systems and behavior expectations served important functions to support law and order in a more traditional sense. Those systems were complete with clear divisions between "right versus wrong" and "us versus them" that rarely consider the social developments of an emerging global community more typical of modern society.

A reliance on social and cultural markers from a religious group as the primary label for establishing personal identity of human beings easily sets followers up to believe that anyone with different faith-based beliefs and/or practices from their own are "outsiders." This might have been very helpful for recognizing potential threats for our ancestors in hunter-gatherer and isolated farming communities, but a more globally connected human race does *not* benefit from these mental shortcuts any longer.

In a more global community, a reliance on these familiar markers of social and/or cultural identity from the Old World only sets the tone for an "us versus them" mindset. That positions people to make the thinking error of *scarcity bias* discussed earlier. An insistence on perceived scarcity will eventually develop into dehumanization of other social and cultural groups—where they are "othered" and treated as unworthy of social acceptance and even less worthy of available resources. This often continues until one group becomes objectified to the degree that violence towards them is accepted. In fact, this is the basis for the bloodiest wars in human history—The Crusades, World War I and II, extermination of indigenous Americans, etc.

Reliance on these cultural markers from isolated farming communities of the Old World as the primary tool for recognizing "in-group status" is simply no longer effective or even beneficial for health and happiness today. However, effective models for meaningful connection to other people and the natural world are still very adaptive and health promoting. The importance lies in those models allowing space for all parties to affiliate with their own social and cultural identity as reflects their authentic personhood. As soon as a group claims their model to be the only effective model for meaningful connection, it is practically inevitable that it will eventually lead to "othering" and ultimately violence.

The problem is that throughout history, there has been *very little* guidance for boys and men about how to create meaningful social connections beyond the traditional roles of warrior and hunter in the Old World—now known as the roles of *protector and provider* in modern society. Thus there are a few behavior expectations about what to do in order to access the social influence available to those roles, but mostly what *not* to do. Even in cases where boys have rich friendships with other boys in childhood, studies show that social pressure to avoid close connection with other males (socially policed as a sign of homosexual tendencies) tends to pull those friendships apart the more men step into those provider and protector roles required for being a "real man" in adulthood.[133]

Because of this social pressure to stay within the lines of traditional manhood, men tend to avoid the emotional vulnerability required for more authentic connection with other males and instead, prefer building more surface level connection based on shared interests in the outside world (sports, work, politics), exchanging jokes, and playful "ribbing/roasting," as well as practical advice-seeking.[134]

If you love a man, does this now remind you of their first response to your emotional reactions when you would *prefer* they "just listen?" It's *not* that men don't care or wouldn't want to participate in this intimate social experience with their partner, but it's almost impossible for most adult men to see this as a healthy and normal opportunity for maintaining trust and connection as a "real man," even in close relationships. In fact, this concept is foreign to most men based on personal experiences with the behavior expectations and belief systems of traditional manhood. Many believe that it is "a sign of weakness" that should be avoided due to the belief that if a man is not actively rescuing a loved one from their pain, then this reflects personal failure in regard to the *protector role*. All the while, this loved one just needs space to be heard, understood, and supported unconditionally so they can be empowered to solve their *own* problems!

This lack of access to a full range of available human skill sets has left most men in modern society open to scarcity bias, social isolation, and resulting chronic health issues—sometimes

133   Keddie, A. (2003). Little boys: Tomorrow's macho lads. *Discourse: Studies in the Cultural politics of Education*, 24(3), 289–306. doi:10.1080/0159630032000172498
134   Garfield, R. (2015). Breaking the male code: Unlocking the power of friendship. New York, NY: Gotham

even active participation in hurting the vulnerable community members who ultimately rely on them for protection with the relative power and influence available from male privilege.

Despite a history of violent conflict between the different organized religions of the world, research has shown that spiritual and faith-based practices come with significant benefits to quality of life and a personal sense of happiness.[135] This section will help you see *why*, then we will discuss how *you* can use these natural solutions that have always been a basic part of human life.

When most Westerners think about meditation, they tend to imagine a very traditional Zen Buddhism setting where practitioners sit on a pillow and "clear their mind" for long periods of time. This assumption is downright intimidating for most men because it seems so *different* from anything they are taught today in a fast-paced Western European culture that prioritizes productivity! Realistically, meditation is a practice that is focused on sharpening skills related to three main areas— controlling *focus* of personal attention, *awareness* of the present moment, and personal control over the relaxation response of our mind and body.[136]

Each organized religion tends to have their own practices provided within the context of distinct cultural expectations, so most people are surprised to learn that each unique methodology from different disciplines actually get the *same* benefits to

135   Witter, R., Stock, W., Okun, M., and Haring, M. (1985). Religion and Subjective Well-Being in Adulthood: A Quantitative Synthesis. *Review of Religious Research, 26*(4), 332-342. doi:10.2307/3511048
136   Awasthi B. (2013). Issues and perspectives in meditation research: in search for a definition. *Frontiers in psychology, 3*, 613. https://doi.org/10.3389/fpsyg.2012.00613

promoting health and wellness as found in meditation.[137] Studies using magnetic resonance imaging (fMRI) scans to look at the brainwaves of nuns in prayer versus Buddhist monks in meditation has found that in virtually the same way as prayer, a practice of meditation produces the *same brain waves* that signal stimulation of the resting/healing systems of the body in a *parasympathetic (resting) state.* [138]

The good news is that people can reduce—even eliminate the negative health outcomes from living in modern society by reclaiming control over the stimulation of our parasympathetic nervous system for rest/digest/recover. A regular practice of prayer or meditation provides the space to consciously rehearse these internal states that, in turn, will lower blood pressure to improve cardiovascular health, increase testosterone to promote physical strength and confidence, increase serotonin to decrease depression and anxiety symptoms, increase sex drive, improve critical thinking and executive decision-making, improve immune function, decrease general inflammation to improve joint pain, stimulate the body's natural recovery and self-healing systems and even slow down the aging process.[139]

Research studies have closely investigated these connections between faith-based practices and longevity to find that in fact,

137   Vieten, C., Amorok, T., Schlitz, M. (2008). Many paths, one mountain: An integral approach to the science of transformation. *The Meaning of Life in the 21st Century: Tensions Among Science, Religion, and Experience.*
138   Josipovic, Z. (2010). Duality and nonduality in meditation research. *Consciousness and Cognition,* 19, 1119–1121.
139   Alda, M., Puebla-Guedea, M., Rodero, B., Demarzo, M., Montero-Marin, J., Roca, M., and Garcia-Campayo, J. (2016). Zen meditation, Length of Telomeres, and the Role of Experiential Avoidance and Compassion. *Mindfulness,* 7, 651–659. https://doi.org/10.1007/s12671-016-0500-5

people of faith live longer and healthier lives—by *four years* to be exact![140]

Whether you want to call it "prayer" or "meditation," the self-regulation skills commonly taught as a part of faith-based practice literally interrupt the human stress response to redirect personal energy toward the mind and body's recovery and self-healing processes by stimulating the parasympathetic nervous system. Meditation and prayer are practices that we can learn on our own as individuals, but what do we do about our everyday relationships and interacting with the world as a social being?

Meditation and prayer are great, but how you live your life is the *real* practice and *no* human can live their *whole life* spent in mediation or prayer! Even a Buddhist Monk who spends much of their day in meditation still lives in a monastery with other monks to maintain meaningful connection to a community.

This tends to be where things get very tricky for men because the preparation from traditional manhood teaches men belief systems and behaviors that all but lock them into positions of extreme independence, emotional cut off, repression of personal needs, hyper-competition with others in a cognitive error of scarcity bias and of course, an overreliance on anger as fuel for motivation. This creates even more pressure on the human body and mind because it remains stuck in the fight/flight of the sympathetic nervous system. This leaves men wide open to chronic self-neglect, mental health problems, relationship failure and compulsive self-soothing through numbing with escapism, …instead of leaning into the safety of social relationships as female community members are socially-trained and culturally

---

140   Wallace, L. E., Anthony, R., End, C., M., Way, B., W. (2019). Does religion stave off the grave? Religious affiliation in one's obituary and longevity. *Social Psychological and Personality Science, 10*(5), 662-670. https://doi.org/10.1177/1948550618779820

encouraged to do. This has been the foundation for the spiking rates of suicide, overdoses, and alcohol toxicity that together reflect *deaths of despair*—the fatality group of young to middle-aged men who self-destruct so much more commonly in modern society that it has decreased the life expectancy of men considerably in the last century relative to women.

Since human beings have *always* been such *social* animals, these relational/social barriers *must* be interrupted for men to heal themselves. Only then will they have a chance to use a position of relative social influence to serve and protect an emerging global community—as has *always* been central to a man's sacred obligations to the human race.

Participation with a healthy faith-based community also tends to create structured space for the healing properties of "community service." The healing power of *community service* is another example of commonly held knowledge that is generally shared by the major religions of the world—from the Judeo-Christian religions of Europe to denominations of Buddhism in Asia. In fact, this active engagement in a process of serving with our gifts/dharma is perhaps the *most* effective way as human beings to actively remind our mind and body that we are indeed a valued part of our community. To put it quite simply, the experience of giving is so effective at promoting healing because we get to experience this unconditional value *personally* through active participation in meaningful relationships with community members. This might sound foreign in modern society, but this is still within reach today when people learn and apply the skills required to collaborate with community members in shared experiences towards mutual values/goals. Over time, these experiences develop the foundation for a meaningful relationship based on unconditional acceptance of authentic self—rather than seeking validation or approval for a "self-identity" built on a foundation of traditional manhood markers.

Not surprisingly, this is where those belief systems and behavior expectations from traditional manhood create barriers yet again because "community service" does *not* involve earning money to buy the material goods that men are commonly misled to believe are indications of "being successful" in regard to personal success and happiness. Traditional manhood expectations easily make community service seem "unproductive" or even "women's work" due to a focus on caretaking in a relatively low power position, so it tends to be devalued as a "waste of valuable time," or even a sign of femininity that reflects grounds for rejection as a "real man."

Community service in formal settings has an important place in society, but what if you could access these benefits to personal health and happiness by creating intentional and healthy relationships with the people you engage with on a *daily basis*? This is where it gets interesting regarding the personal health benefits of a meaningful relationship. These health benefits are very similar, if not identical to those from faith-based and spiritual practices, where the mind is capable of stimulating a *parasympathetic resting state* to support recovery and healing in the body.

Rather than focusing solely on self-regulation—as with meditation and prayer that can only happen in social isolation—most men would benefit *greatly* from stimulating the *parasympathetic resting state* in social relationships. In fact, this is the missing link for most men due to the social and cultural barriers established by traditional manhood belief systems and behavior expectations. The experience of communicating with a loved one where the speaker is being accepted unconditionally creates the process of mutual soothing discussed earlier, where this experience of social safety in the face of personal vulnerability stimulates the pathways of healing and recovery associated with the parasympathetic nervous system (as with meditation and prayer) but can be accessed at any time we are with other people. These are the same healing pathways of the body and mind that are left over from a reliance of our early human ancestors on important social connections for survival of our species.

Studies show that the naturally-occurring healing chemicals from the parasympathetic nervous system are released into the bloodstream when we experience safe connection and love—whether this takes place inside the context of an officially recognized faith-based community—or not. The only requirement is that we can accept each other with unconditional support and nonjudgment in this state of personal unrest—in the same way that all organized religions through the world pose that there is a loving piece of "source energy" or "grace" that provides healing for followers in times of stress or need.

This happens when a chemical called "oxytocin"—the "bonding chemical"—is released in the brain. In a similar way that meditation stimulates the healing properties of the body, the sharing of supportive and honest care between people *also* triggers the parasympathetic resting state to naturally soothe and relieve stress in the mind and body. This is triggered with the release of oxytocin in the brain when we receive warmth and care from another person while we are in a state of pain or fear. This experience is how people develop greater trust in a relationship as a safe place, where we learn to expect a given relationship as a "secure base" associated with basic needs of social safety and acceptance.[141] This has *always* been central for the survival of human beings since our early ancestors.

141   Tatkin, S. (2011). *Wired for love: How understanding your partner's brain and attachment style can help you defuse conflict and build a secure relationship.* Oakland, CA: New Harbinger Publications.

While a personal practice of meditation and prayer is helpful for learning to regulate our own body and mind, healthy relationships are the other half of the "secret sauce" for human beings. They make it possible for us to promote healing with each other through mutual experiences that create space for unconditional acceptance that builds trust, understanding, and a resulting sense of safety and security. Further, this healing experience of trust and understanding with others creates a self-reinforced feedback loop, where the release of oxytocin makes it easier for both parties in the relationship to practice even more compassion to facilitate greater understanding and trust which, in turn, results in the release of more oxytocin to continue stimulating the healing properties of the parasympathetic nervous system.[142] This self-fed loop is the invisible connection between loved ones, where *generosity* and *kindness* continues building on itself in loving and supportive relationships to facilitate a mutual desire to remain connected between both parties.

A loving and supportive relationship has been tied to the same health benefits found in meditation (lower blood pressure, improved immune support, slower aging, etc.), but with the added benefits of community reinforcement and social connection. This increases social bonding and serves to reinforce safety in the relationship (in both platonic and sexual relationships), which is a buffer against the social isolation that plagues many men today. The addition of a trusting relationship only serves to expand personal health benefits to include a reduction in cravings for addictive behavior (proven for food,

142   Moberg, K. U., Handlin, L., Tackett, K., K., Petersson, M. (2019). Oxytocin is a principal hormone that exerts part of its effects by active fragments. *Medical Hypotheses, 113*, https://doi.org/10.1016/j. mehy.2019.109394.

alcohol, and nicotine)[143], an increase in protective instincts for loved ones[144] and even an increase in sexual arousal between romantic partners.[145]

A connection to our natural world can also provide many of the personal health benefits associated with faith-based practices and healthy relationships. When we create a safe and reliable connection with an animal who is not human, this becomes another source of self-regulation, healing, and recovery. Most people have experienced this firsthand with a pet or when working closely with domestic (maybe even wild) animals, but it has not been studied until recently largely due to old political forces in the social and cultural expectations from organized religion that have criticized this type of viewpoint as "blasphemous."

The Japanese have long practiced "Forest Bathing," an experience of mindfulness that takes place in a forest setting. Studies show that the simple act of inhaling the natural chemicals given off by plants in the forest increases the number of "natural killer cells" that support our immune system in fighting off bacteria, viruses, and cancer cells.[146]

143   Uvnäs-Moberg, K., Handlin, L., and Petersson, M. (2015). Self-soothing behaviors with particular reference to oxytocin release induced by non-noxious sensory stimulation. *Frontiers in psychology*, 5, 1529. https://doi.org/10.3389/fpsyg.2014.01529

144   De Dreu, C., K., Carsten and Greer, Lindred and Handgraaf, Michel and Shalvi, Shaul and van Kleef, Gerben and Baas, Matthijs and Velden, Femke and Dijk, Eric and Feith, Sander. (2010). The Neuropeptide Oxytocin Regulates Parochial Altruism in Intergroup Conflict Among Humans. *Science*,328, 1408-11. 10.1126/science.1189047

145   Magon, N., and Kalra, S. (2011). The orgasmic history of oxytocin: Love, lust, and labor. *Indian journal of endocrinology and metabolism*, 15 Suppl 3(Suppl3), S156–S161. https://doi.org/10.4103/2230-8210.84851

146   Hansen, M. M., Jones, R., and Tocchini, K. (2017). Shinrin-Yoku (Forest Bathing) and Nature Therapy: A State-of-the-Art Review. *International journal of environmental research and public health*, 14(8), 851. https://doi.org/10.3390/ijerph14080851

A relatively new field of counseling psychology called "Ecopsychology" is studying this connection between our personal health and well-being to a greater connection with our natural world. Even though this is a relatively new field in Western science, research studies have already proven that time in nature has the following benefits: lowers blood pressure, lowers cortisol levels, reduces arousal of nervous system associated with anxiety symptoms, improves immune system function, increases self-esteem, improves mood, and reduces the harmful effects of isolation.[147]

Are you seeing the connections here between healing in a community setting and the universal similarities between belief systems in the major religions of the world? A pattern is emerging where the solutions to personal health and happiness lie in our ability to exist as our authentic self while we participate meaningfully in healthy relationships defined by unconditional love and support. This breathes love, contentment, and gratitude into the people around us and when we are all operating from a position of unconditional love, service, and empowerment, this connects all members of a community to "The Source of Life."

This type of connection creates an ideal setting for personal health and happiness through mutual trust and safety, which allows each person to bring down the defenses of the *ego* that blocks access to true self. This allows each human being to exist in the world as they are—unattached to past regrets or anxious thoughts about the future—beautiful and unique in their own way with their own unique values, gifts, and passions—one small part of an intricate web of biodiversity that human beings

---

147   Franco, L. S., Shanahan, D. F., and Fuller, R. A. (2017). A Review of the Benefits of Nature Experiences: More Than Meets the Eye. *International journal of environmental research and public health*, 14(8), 864. https://doi. org/10.3390/ijerph14080864

have always relied on for dynamic group problem solving to facilitate the success of humankind.

CHAPTER 8: LIVING WITH PURPOSE IN MODERN SOCIETY

———

Most men think about their "purpose" as making a certain amount of money, attaining a high level of professional achievement, or otherwise receiving some "stamp of approval" from the outside world as a sign of exceptionalism. This has its roots in the original hunter/provider role that elevates the priority of collecting material resources so there is no need to rely on anyone else for meeting basic needs of self and loved ones. Financial security is important to a point, but the sole focus of chasing money and power as a sign of success or happiness is a set-up for a rat race that only ends in poor health, low-quality relationships, lower health outcomes for those closest to us, social isolation, low life satisfaction for ourselves and even violence and an early death.

Rather than getting stuck trying to apply this Old World formula to modern society, it is much more helpful to consider the following areas—personal integrity, gifts, and passions—as the foundation for a realistic, practical and scientifically sound focus for daily life that is both functional for meeting human needs, as well as adaptive in a community setting.

Integrity

Integrity is a collection of core values that guide personal intentions for daily decision-making and behavior choices. These come from a set of morals and ethics that are distinct to *you* as a human being who is a unique and valuable part of a community/tribe/family that relies on enough diversity in its ranks to solve dynamic problems. As the old wisdom goes, "it takes all kinds," and *this is why*! A community can only be as effective as the problems it can solve, so the more variation that exists in the ranks, the more adaptive and functional a community can be in its collective response to the chaos of the natural world.

Gifts

Everyone has their own set of *knowledge, skills* and *resources* that make up their "gifts"—tools that are of value to human life in community settings. Whether this involves physical size and stamina that can be used for labor to meet community needs, a brain that is good at hyperfocusing on patterns/analytics to solve important problems, or a collection of other assets that can be used for meeting the basic needs of community members, every person has a *unique* collection of knowledge, skills, and resources to bring to bear.

Gifts are sometimes *inherited* (physical size, raw intelligence, or socioeconomic advantage), *taught* (family trades) or *learned through hardship*. It is important to note *male privilege* as a force of social influence relative to women is in and of itself a *resource* that makes up a part of this collection of gifts for men to meaningfully serve their community.

Passions

Every person also has a unique set of personal interests that are naturally a source of passion, motivation, and excitement. When people apply these natural passions with the leverage available from a set of gifts in a direction that also meets their integrity, people are capable of intense and productive focus for long periods of time. It is nice to be *proficient* at the activities required to engage in an experience, but if we have enough passion for it and it also meets our *integrity,* people often do the hard work of learning the required skill sets sooner than later because they are bringing so much personal energy to the experience.

This ideal combination of using our gifts and passions driven by personal integrity creates a state of hyperfocus where someone is "all in"—whether this is working with our hands in soil, climbing a mountain, planning strategies for business execution in the modern market or creating technological innovation. This naturally enjoyable and productive frame of mind is an optimal state for productivity referred to the psychology field as a "flow state"[148]—where the mind and body is highly productive and at peace at the same time, allowing life satisfaction to flow by addressing needs of productivity and simultaneously stimulating the stress reduction benefits from the parasympathetic nervous system.[149]

It is important to remember that just because someone is "gifted" in a particular area for *whatever* reason, this doesn't mean that the intended use of these gifts meets a personal sense of *integrity,* or that someone has enough passion to execute at the required level.

There are many different options out there for how we will spend our time and why in modern society, not to mention the competing forces of big business that aim to convince community members to pledge allegiance to *their* values, rather than operate by our own moral code. There is also the problem of relying on social isolation and avoiding group cooperation, which is a glaring blind spot for most men and boys because of being confined by the rigid social and cultural expectations of traditional manhood.

148   Gold, J., and Ciorciari, J. (2020). A Review on the Role of the Neuroscience of Flow States in the Modern World. *Behavioral sciences (Basel, Switzerland), 10*(9), 137. https://doi.org/10.3390/bs10090137
149   Csikszentmihalyi, M. (1997). *The masterminds' series. Finding flow: The psychology of engagement with everyday life.* Basic Books.

Between men being cut off from their *purpose* by the forces of modern society and then separated from meeting the basic social needs for a *human being,* men and boys are being left out to dry in a way that is convincing many of them to redirect their anger and hostility back towards themselves or even other community members. This keeps men reliant on those same belief systems and strategies that commonly end in chronic self-neglect, compulsively seeking to escape with substance use or high-risk behavior and culminating in the recent spike in deaths of despair.

The social influence from male privilege and even the physical prowess leftover in male DNA is not "toxic," but it *will* make men sick if the user does not learn to share it meaningfully and respectfully with other community members in a way that empowers *their* gifts. Going back to the teachings of Jesus Christ and Buddha alike, the journey of learning to separate true self from a socially constructed identity is required. Each person must first unlearn these cultural trappings in order to make room for re-learning how to be a *good human.* It is from this position of "abundance" that people are best positioned to meaningfully share their unique gifts with the world, resulting in mutual empowerment while minimizing risk of harm.

Since it is so common for men to get cut off from a sense of purpose in modern society by the social and cultural expectations of the Old World in a more global and interconnected community, men must make their *own* efforts to reintroduce *themselves* to a more personal understanding of purpose—or risk losing their personal integrity to the institutions that govern our communities.

It is easy to see why men have been prepared for leadership positions through the process of evolution. Since men are not capable of giving birth and women are, this has allowed men the space to focus efforts outside of the home towards the unknown of the horizon and wonder, "How can I make sure my community is provided for and my pregnant wife is safe?"

One of the most important traits of a good leader is the ability to make the best decisions with the information available to facilitate a plan of execution that benefits the community. Since men have been able to operate outside of the home as an independent agent since the inception of the human race, men not only developed the physical leverage and power to take on trials and tribulations in the outside world but have also been formally given legal leverage until very recently. Over the course of human history, the social and cultural expectations for men versus women have taken shape as a response to these male advantages in the form of *male privilege* so that communities could make sure "there are not too many cooks in the kitchen."

Men have *always* been the primary shepherds and guardians of our communities, but now the standards of traditional manhood that used to be so helpful tend to create barriers to fulfilling this sacred obligation in an emerging global community. How are men supposed to create a personal sense of purpose in their own communities to facilitate this restorative process if they are not taught the social and communication skills required to engage adequately? It would be *impossible!*

The answers lie in the ability to connect with self and others using a full range of emotional experiences so this information can be used to keep two main forces in balance—first, for alignment with a personal sense of purpose and second, to protect connection in prioritized social relationships. A healthy balance between these human needs steers daily behavior towards serving our community meaningfully with a personal sense of *purpose,* while doing so in a way that also builds trust, understanding and connection with other community members so we can empower them as well-informed and benevolent leaders.

The good news is that it is not "rocket science"—in fact, it is very straight-forward "human science" that guides the use of these new tools in a way that unlocks access to the rest of our own humanity, as well as the safety and healing of our community members through the power of love, rather than the love of power. From this position, we can facilitate restorative relationships that empower vulnerable community members to develop more autonomy, who can then do the same for others. All of the while, these shared experiences with community members stimulate a mutual process of healing and recovery by way of the parasympathetic nervous system for *all* community members who are participating.

This social experience allows space for all parties involved to break free from the rigid confines of traditional gender expectations to access authentic self-identity, be accepted unconditionally as we truly are, then satisfy any previously unmet physical and mental health needs as a human being. This process promotes sustainability for relationships by keeping them healthy and cohesive since everybody's basic human needs are respected.

This not only allows people to maintain trust in their community because good leaders must constantly seek active consent of their community served, but also maximizes our use of available assets by tapping into a greater variation of resources. When the effort is toward mutual goals to promote shared integrity, people naturally *want* to invest their passions and gifts because they feel honored, respected, and productive in that personal experience. Not only do these practices keep relationships together for the "right reasons," but this type of process also yields the most adaptive problem solving for taking on the chaos of the natural world because a community can now bring *all* of its available fruit to bear against the dynamic problem at hand—as human beings have always done.

This concept sounds great to most people because we are literally programmed for it by our DNA. But the difficult part comes with realistic application, where belief systems and behavioral habits from the Old World come into direct conflict both internally against the needs of true self, as well as with other people who come from different cultural groups who are only very recently coming into such direct contact with each other in a more global community. These types of situations often feel tense and uncomfortable, which tends to be tricky for men because they are rarely encouraged to explore emotional states beyond anger. This blocks most men from accessing the natural wisdom from emotional experiences that is essential for facilitating personal interactions with others that build trust, increase depth of understanding,   optimize productivity and of course, protect healthy connections between community members.

How are men supposed to do this when they are taught as boys to be so reliant on the behaviors and belief systems from traditional manhood that provide short-term access to social influence and resources, but at the cost of restricting social and emotional wisdom?

Due to the pressures of traditional manhood, most boys are socialized from an early age to avoid what are essentially the requirements for intimacy in relationships—vulnerability, a full range of emotional intelligence, and the ability to express personal pain and/or fear.[150] This sets men up for difficulty with

---

150   Way, N. (2011). Deep secrets: Boys' friendships and the crisis of connection. Cambridge, MA: Harvard University Press. doi:10.4159/harvard.9780674061361

relationships in adulthood because some of the basic required social and emotional skill sets are missing.[151] Since this is such a significant gap for most men, the next chapter will be about increasing emotional intelligence so you can use the required social skills to put it all together.

Purpose Exercise

Passions

What do you *naturally* enjoy doing? These might be personal *hobbies* or parts of your *job* that are especially *interesting*. If nothing comes to mind, what did you do before life "took over?" You might have to go back to **childhood** memories to access these activities:

_____

_____

_____

_____

_____

---

151   O'Neil, J. M. (2015). Men's gender role conflict: Psychological costs, consequences, and an agenda for change. Washington, DC: American Psychological Association

Gifts/Talents

What are you *good* at? What can you do that creates *value* – either through group effort or on your own? This might be more *physical, mental, practical,* or *creative* – depending on each *unique* person:

_____

_____

_____

_____

_____

Integrity

What are your Core Values?

1.   Jot down as many personal values that you admire and want to represent in your life that meet your own Integrity

_____

_____

2.   After you have listed at least 15 values, group the items into a few main categories – 5 max

_____

_____

3.   Name these main categories of values with the character trait that best summarizes each category from #2 best

_____

_____

Below you will find a "A Guide for the Balanced Man." As you are considering how to expand your sense of humanity to seek a healthy balance for self-identity and social relationships, feel free to refer to the table below as you plan to expand on your "comfort zone" so you can get some different results that put you on a more authentic track to your full humanity:

Traditional Manhood versus Balanced Manhood

Traditional Manhood	Balanced Manhood
Trying to influence or control the behavior of others with higher level of personal influence/power	Taking a "step back" to value shared influence in relationships by prioritizing mutual trust and respect that allows collective effort
Looking to boost self-esteem and/or status through winning and/or collecting money, influence, or other resources	Self-esteem created through balance of task completion *and* being emotionally available in important relationships
Avoiding tasks inside the home that are traditionally "feminine" (housework, childcare, family social/ medical schedule)	Taking on traditionally "feminine tasks" and valuing those activities—both inside *and* outside of the home
Emotional restriction (except for anger and *maybe h*appy); emotional distance and/ or avoidance of sharing vulnerable feelings openly	Commitment to expressing a full range of emotions— including insecurity, pain, and fear—in a way that builds mutual trust and understanding

Having a "non-relational" mindset towards sex and sexuality	Actively participating in a mutual exchange of emotional safety and respect
Leadership in the face of hard times based on making decisions with very little to no teamwork—failure to utilize collective knowledge of all community members	Stay flexible through hard times—showing respect for other people's thoughts, feelings, and opinion as much as own ideas with servant leadership that optimizes both outcomes and morale of group members
Independence and relying on self, rather than depending on other people	Learning to value teamwork and satisfying group needs in order to maximize resilience
Homophobia, as characterized by fear/anger at LGBTQ+ Identifying people. Also avoiding closeness with other males—relying on females for closeness	Valuing difference and creating personal relationships with people based on mutual respect, care, and accountability regardless of gender presentation or sexual orientation
Using aggression, intimidation, or the manipulation of resources as the preferred method to resolve conflict and/or "get the point across"	Relying on fair compromise and active collaboration that empowers the autonomy all community members at a developmentally appropriate level and at the least—does no harm

CHAPTER 9: EMOTIONAL INTELLIGENCE AS THE "MISSING LINK"

The idea of allowing our emotional experiences to enter into our decision-making process is *not* popular historically. The Greeks and Romans spoke about "stoicism" 5,000 years ago (3000 B.C.), before the rise of Judeo-Christian religion. The *stoic philosophers* saw the potential danger of emotions running wild in the isolated farming communities of the Old World, where impulsive decision-making led community members to make illogical, irrational, and less reliable choices. This created unnecessary risk that disrupted a community's stability in a world that required a lot of structure to operate successfully.

About 4,500 years after introduction from Greek and Roman philosophers, the concept of *stoicism* was reintroduced in the 1600s when it was incorporated by Christianity. Stoicism was considered a practical concept where "The Good Life" is possible when people refuse to be influenced by "passionate states," which were seen as synonymous with unpredictability and chaos—*greed, fear, joy,* and *sorrow.* Instead, they recommended submitting these passionate emotional states to "the will of God" to avoid being drawn off "the righteous path," where unhappiness and lack of life satisfaction was seen as a byproduct of refusing to live according to "God's plan."

This popular concept of *emotional restriction* influenced the work of many popular European writers of the 1600s and 1700s, who drove the Age of Enlightenment and the resulting Scientific Revolution. The popularity of emotional restriction continued on as the scientific method gained more popularity and seemed to reinforce previously held beliefs by past philosophers and religious leaders alike that the presence of emotion decreases the validity and reliability required for seeking truth—at this point echoed as "scientific validation." While the European writers of the Enlightenment and Scientific Revolution were very important to the development of modern science as we know it, they also lacked understanding regarding the important role of emotions as it relates to information processing, group cooperation, healthy relationships and wellness for human beings.

The Industrial Revolution began in Europe in the mid-1700s, then reached the New World in the mid-1800s. This brought economic innovation that required workers to run the factories and with this, new opportunities invited a huge influx of laborers from their isolated farming communities of origin into the newly developed urban areas. Naturally, these newly displaced adults not only sought opportunity for employment, but also for romantic partnership in another social movement called the "Age of Romanticism."

As discussed in Chapter 4, this wave of migration into urban areas created a mixing of people that was not typical for the inhabitants of previously isolated communities. With that mixing also came a newfound social freedom that represented an explosion of romantic themes that were found in arts, music, and architecture. People no longer had to rely on the traditional social and cultural expectations of politically-arranged marriages that were so functional in the isolated farming communities of the Old World. In the newly emerging cities, there were new and different opportunities to make a livelihood, or even find a different sexual partner outside of more traditional politically-arranged partnerships.

The Age of Romanticism popularized unrealistic concepts like "living in eternal romantic bliss" by way of "romantic love" in popular novels of the time. Urban dwellers were quite excited about this concept of romantic love, but keep in mind this has been a very new development for long-term committed relationships relative to the more general timeline of human social and cultural development. Instead, both boys and girls have been prepared for the last hundreds and thousands of years for traditional gender roles that are largely outdated in urban settings and even less so in the fast-paced and globally-connected communities of modern society.

Romantic love became so popular because it feels *good*. However, romantic love was seen as *only* something for mistresses and men trying to have sex with women out of wedlock. Thus these parts of human life were largely seen as off-limits before the Industrial Revolution and have not yet been fully integrated into most people's behavior expectations or belief systems. Realize, the event of an unplanned pregnancy out of wedlock reflected a great danger for throwing off the required level of community structure and stability. This means that while romance was popularized in books, media, and eventually advertising as a concept to sell merchandise, most people in modern society generally have *no* idea how to put sustainable romance into practice. Despite all of the tools available through human methods of communication, we have had little to no realistic exposure through personal experiences or observation.

This cultural history around the dangers of emotional expression—even in romance—have both built and reinforced the behavioral expectations and belief systems for traditional manhood, where the sacred roles of provider and protector must *always* appear independent, emotionless, and dominant. There are many amazing parts of being a man but in some fundamental ways, the belief systems and behavior expectations are in dire need of an update from the behavior expectations and belief systems of traditional manhood reflected by the Old World.

In modern society, it has become clear that emotions are much more than potential barriers to rational thought. While emotional experiences *can* impede reason, this is not actually a bad thing until it actually brings harm to someone. In fact, emotional experiences are very important sources of personal wisdom that guide moment to moment decision-making to support the ongoing balance between meeting a sense of personal integrity rooted in self-identity and reinforcing meaningful social connection.

When it comes to emotional intelligence, many men are surprised to realize the depth and range of experiences available, how important emotions are to unlocking personal wisdom, as well as building trust, connection, and intimacy with others. Emotions are the "inside look" into our personal wants and needs, as well as guidance regarding how to interact with others through tension in a way that not only resolves conflict productively, but also creates deeper levels of understanding, connection, and trust with the people who make up our "love and belonging needs" so these important connections can be protected.

The phrase "love and belonging needs" was popularized by the famous American Psychologist Abraham Maslow who is credited with "Maslow's Hierarchy of Needs,"[152] a foundational concept for human development that is still taught today at introductory levels throughout every field of modern psychology and sociology. *Maslow's Hierarchy of Needs* identified and

---

[152]   Maslow, A. H. (1968). *Toward a psychology of being.* New York: Van Nostrand Reinhold Co.

prioritized the different categories of human needs—with basic needs of food, water, and shelter as the most essential for survival, then "safety needs" as the second priority, and finally *love and belonging needs* was believed to be third on the list.

Maslow introduced what has been a valuable concept for the development of modern psychology over the last 60 years, but the specific placement of *love and belonging needs* actually appears to be *incorrect* given more modern research. There is a great deal of convincing evidence since Maslow's work that shows the social needs of *love and belonging* are *much* more essential to healthy and successful human life than originally believed!

Harry Harlow was a researcher who studied primates in the 1960s and 1970s. His experiments showed that when baby monkeys were given the opportunity to choose between a "metal wire caretaker surrogate" with food and water for physical sustenance, or a "warm caretaker surrogate" with no food or water, that the baby monkeys would regularly choose the *warm mom surrogate* to experience the sensation of "cuddling." Rather than choose the *wire mom surrogate* and receive basic nutritional needs, the baby monkeys consistently chose the option that felt like the physical presence a warm-blooded animal, even if this meant also choosing dehydration and malnourishment. In fact, the research had to be cut off prematurely due to the baby monkeys becoming dehydrated and malnourished, rather than spend time with the *wire mom surrogate* to meet nutritional needs and face the even *more* stressful experience of social isolation.[153]

---

153   Harlow, H. F., and Suomi, S. J. (1971). Social recovery by isolation-reared monkeys. *Proceedings of the National Academy of Sciences of the United States of America*, 68(7), 1534–1538. https://doi.org/10.1073/pnas.68.7.1534

In light of what we know about the physical breakdown caused by the stress response of the sympathetic nervous system and the natural healing properties of the parasympathetic nervous system, this is probably not a surprise to hear! Even these rhesus monkeys—with considerably less complex social dynamics and resulting needs for neurological development—found a greater sense of personal safety in *love and belonging*, rather than the "basic physical needs" or "safety needs" as identified by Maslow's Hierarchy of Needs.

In the same vein as the research from Harry Harlow's rhesus monkeys, human babies who experience emotional neglect, yet are provided enough food/water/shelter, will *also* not develop as nature intended. These experiences have been studied and documented at length in newly emerging research over the last few decades around childhood trauma that are directly connected to onset of mental health issues like Post-traumatic Stress Disorder (PTSD), mood disorders, and even personality disorders later in life.[154] In many cases, the negative effects from neglect in studies conducted with kids from Russian orphanages over several decades has shown that prolonged neglect—even *without* any notable firsthand exposure to physical violence—can result in an infant's brain having *significant* developmental delays on a physical level. In cases of more extreme neglect, brain development becomes so derailed from a complete lack of stimulation that there are even cases of infants dying from a "failure to thrive" that is caused by neurological degeneration characteristic of extreme neglect.[155]

154   Bruce, J., Gunnar, M. R., Pears, K. C., and Fisher, P. A. (2013). Early adverse care, stress neurobiology, and prevention science: Lessons learned. *Prevention Science*, 14(3), 247–256.
155   St. Petersburg-USA Orphanage Research Team (2008). The effects of early social-emotional and relationship experience on the development of young orphanage children. The St. Petersburg-USA Orphanage Research Team. *Monographs of the Society for Research in Child Development*, 73(3), vii–295. https://doi.org/10.1111/j.1540-5834.2008.00483.x

In many ways, the expression of emotions—especially vulnerable ones like sadness, insecurity, or fear—is an important part of meaningful communication between human beings. The expression of emotion can be understood as the different notes that make up the shared music of collaborative efforts and social relationships. Emotional expression allows a deeper level of understanding between people so that optimal trust can be gained for effective group problem solving to meet basic needs (food/water/shelter), while maintaining balance with the needs of other community members. This facilitates ongoing connection and safety by ensuring that everyone's needs will be met reliably and respectfully.

Research from an established field of psychology called "Attachment Theory" has shown that a failure to consistently meet the *love and belonging needs* of children results in their growing into adults who do *not* learn how to trust people enough to be vulnerable with them in times of stress—even to be scared or ashamed of their own natural vulnerability as human beings.[156]

When kids grow up with safe, consistent, and emotionally-attuned caregivers as children, this lays the foundation for a "secure attachment style" in adulthood. An adult with a secure attachment style generally holds a personal belief based on previous experiences that life stressors and their resulting emotions—no matter how uncomfortable and upsetting—can be openly and honestly experienced with those around us at no risk of losing social acceptance and even more, with the expectation of active support and caring. This provides the brain with an opportunity for ideal neurological development on a physical level, but also lays the groundwork for success in future relationships. It provides a safe space for development

156   Johnson, S. M. (2019). *Attachment theory in practice.* Guilford Press.

of self-awareness and emotional regulation, and creates a bed of memories from positive experiences with help-seeking behaviors that continue reinforcing the likelihood of ongoing connection in adaptive and prosocial behavior in adulthood.

Alternately, kids who do not experience warmth and accessibility from their caretakers during painful and/or scary experiences in childhood are most likely to develop an "insecure attachment style." Kids with an insecure attachment style do *not* learn to see other people as reliable in times of stress and this leaves them open to poor self-regulation skills, limited self-awareness, and avoidance of vulnerability.

Since the safe expression of vulnerable emotion is required for emotional self-awareness and facilitating meaningful social connection to others, the avoidant nature of an insecure attachment style tends to continue disrupting relationships into adulthood by continuing to block emotional expression of vulnerability. This "attachment injury" can be healed through active participation in a healthy relationship, but this healing process requires learning some new communication skills so the reader can actively participate in the "corrective emotional experiences." These skills will be shared in greater detail later in this book for use in your own personal toolkit.

In addition to an insecure attachment blocking close social connection to meet *love and belonging needs*, this type of relational disruption also makes it *very* hard to advocate for personal wants and needs in a way that makes other people want to listen. Since there is very little room for a sense of vulnerability, it is common for someone with insecure attachment to be reactive in anger and seek social isolation in times of stress, since this feels safer and more functional than relying on other people given previous experiences where caretakers were not consistently reliable and, in some cases, could not happen safely.

While anger certainly has its place, the open expression of anger—especially when accompanied by "physical outbursts"—tends to feel threatening for other people. As a result, those vulnerable emotions that are supposed to be a key to human bonding can go in the other direction when they are repressed into the unconscious—where they build negative pressure until they eventually become fuel for unregulated anger and social isolation. This makes it even harder for people to connect with others and/or play an active role in meeting basic social needs. This meaningful and functional connection is required to satisfy the basic human needs of social connection, as well as to facilitate effective community leadership through collaborative group problem solving.

Emotions have not been popular historically as a source of personal wisdom and especially amongst men, but work in a relatively new field of psychology called "Emotional Intelligence" has shown that emotional experiences come with their *own* knowledge related directly to the essential goal of maintaining a meaningful connection with others and minimizing the risk of violence—whether through dialogue, productive conflict resolution or group collaboration.[157]

In order to develop a strong skill set in emotional intelligence, a person must be able to practice "empathy" with other people during social interactions. Empathy is the experience of mutual understanding and trust required to be perceived as an ally (on the "same team") who intends to respect another person's needs and worldview. These communication and social skills are essential for meeting basic needs as a fundamentally social species, as well as maintaining healthy boundaries with our *own* personal needs so we can be meaningfully valued as well.

---

157   Goleman, D. (1998). *Working with emotional intelligence.* New York: Bantam Books.

This dynamic balance between personal needs and social needs ensures ongoing connection and safety because it allows people to expect fair treatment in their community.

This is not to say that emotional expression is *always* "the answer;" studies clearly show that when people are at their *most* emotional, people are also at their *least* rational.[158] So, how do these emotions make us more *intelligent*? From a black and white perspective on rationality, emotions *do* tend to pull people away from "reason," but this doesn't mean feelings are less important – in fact, emotions are the "X-Factor."

Life in our natural world is oftentimes chaotic, and therefore is often *not* rational! People also tend to be emotionally reactive, which is "not rational," but it is also reality. The ability to understand and meet our unique personal needs are also not always "rational," but are more about "what makes us tick" as unique human beings. Without consulting our feelings, we would make decisions like machines and when it comes to predicting people's behavior in unpredictable settings, machines actually do an *awful* job of ethical decision-making,[159] the cornerstone of ongoing community cohesion.

An emotional experience is an internal sign that the focus of our current attention is either in line with our wants and needs—or *not*. When it comes to meeting personal needs and desires, emotions are like gauges on the dashboard of a car that tell us when an experience is either more or less aligned with

158   Jung, N., Wranke, C., Hamburger, K., and Knauff, M. (2014). How emotions affect logical reasoning: evidence from experiments with mood-manipulated participants, spider phobics, and people with exam anxiety. *Frontiers in psychology*, 5, 570. https://doi.org/10.3389/fpsyg.2014.00570
159   Kavathatzopoulos I., Asai R. (2013) Can Machines Make Ethical Decisions? In: Papadopoulos H., Andreou A.S., Iliadis L., Maglogiannis I. (eds) Artificial Intelligence Applications and Innovations. AIAI 2013. IFIP Advances in Information and Communication Technology, vol 412. Springer, Berlin, Heidelberg. https://doi.org/10.1007/978-3-642-41142-7_70

our personal agenda. They don't tell us specifically what "the problem" is, but when we slow down enough to notice these emotional gauges for what they are, we can gather the important information available for better decision-making—both in social and personal life.

So even though emotions have not been historically popular, especially for men and leaders, it turns out that the more someone is able to develop a full range of emotional intelligence, the more likely they will be able to understand the unique perspectives of each party and the multiple sources of information available from those perspectives. From here, a facilitator can gain an optimal level of trust in social relationships by honoring each individual's worldview. This not only allows more dynamic problem solving because *all* available information and skills from each group member can be brought to bear for problem solving, but this also promotes cohesion within the social group because each member's sense of personal integrity can be respected through an experience of shared meaning-making.

People with a high level of emotional intelligence can do this fluidly in the moment while in day-to-day interactions with others to better meet their own needs, honor the personal needs of others, and maintain healthy and supportive relationships with those whom they come into contact with. However, due to the barriers presented by belief systems and behavior expectations from traditional manhood in accessing male privilege, most boys are not "schooled" in the way of emotional intelligence like female peers. As a result, most boys are left woefully under-prepared for leadership positions, not to mention the ability to meet basic social needs in order to live a satisfying life as a human being.

Over time, it can be very difficult for someone who has enough practice repressing and pushing down these emotions to consider a different way of interacting with the world, as well as with other people. This is a common thought for someone without these skill sets since it can seem so unfamiliar, but it is far from impossible!

With this said, the process of learning to access a full range of emotional intelligence *does* require new skills for most men that must be learned through personal experiences which are often outside of the familiar comfort zone. Just like exercising the body for physical fitness, a person who desires to grow *must* be willing to practice the skills of focus towards a progressive overload of this familiar baseline for growth. Despite what you might have been taught about having "no fear" as a sign of courage, it is this very willingness to leave one's comfort zone to actively engage despite feeling the fear that *real* bravery is all about.

Are you telling me David wasn't scared to face Goliath—a giant armed soldier—with a slingshot? I am almost *sure* he was, but the story goes that he did it anyways! Beyond any literal interpretations of this story from the Old Testament, let this also be a clear example that *courage is not the absence of fear—* instead, *courage is feeling scared and in the face of this fear, going for it.*

However, rather than learning to accept uncomfortable emotions as a natural human experience and harnessing this source of personal wisdom in modern society, men are commonly taught to suppress those uncomfortable emotions. Instead, men are taught to nurture skill sets that can be traded for monetary value in a local economy to satisfy the roles of financial provider. These abilities commonly become the primary focus of adulthood as boys grow into men, rather than maintaining an adequate focus on other important human needs like social belonging, self-esteem, personal safety, etc. The missing link here for most men is emotional intelligence, which is *rarely* taught in a way that allows men and boys to meet their human needs.

Boys are encouraged to keep emotions restricted as a nuisance to "rational decision-making" for the most part, except where anger can be used for personal motivation or the control of other people's behavior if this is "required to get the job done." Beyond the expression of anger towards self and others, boys and men are rarely given much more guidance regarding human emotional life. Anger is certainly an important emotion to harness, but an overreliance on anger is a set-up for *disaster*.

This type of social training does well to prepare young hunters (providers) and warriors (protectors) for battle or hunting that one might expect from a "strong man" as defined by traditional manhood, but it does *not* prepare males for the other essential roles available in human life as a meaningful part of modern society, and especially as a global community takes shape. In fact, these very common childhood experiences that prepare boys for traditional manhood—like emotional restriction, over-reliance on anger as a tool, fierce independence, a willingness to do *anything* to win, avoidance of vulnerability, and devaluing "femininity"—are closely linked to *insecure attachment styles* for boys[160] that commonly end in relationship difficulties, an absence of healthy self-soothing, and even makes interpersonal violence more likely.[161] In many ways, these typical

160   Schwartz, J. P., Waldo, M., and Higgins, A. J. (2004). Attachment styles: Relationships to masculine gender role conflict in college men. *Psychology of Men and Masculinity,* 5(2), 143-146. doi:10.1037/1524-9220.5.2.143

161   Mahalik, J. R., Aldarondo, E., Gilbert-Gokhale, S., and Shore, E. (2005). The role of insecure attachment and gender role stress in predicting controlling behaviors in men who batter. *Journal of Interpersonal Violence,* 20(5), 617–631. doi:10.1177/0886260504269688

experiences of boys getting taught to "man up" separates them from their own humanity—as well as the humanity of others.

The fact of the matter is that human beings need social safety to be happy and healthy—regardless of gender. In order to create a meaningful sense of safety, the most vulnerable emotions of fear, insecurity, and shame must be safe and open for direct expression. The less someone is able to express these vulnerable emotions as intended, the more stressed-out the mind and body becomes as they are pushed out of conscious awareness, stimulating the "fight/flight" of the sympathetic nervous system and creating a never-ending cycle of irritability, social isolation and escapism that commonly ends in chronic illness and relationship failure.

The more people have warm and predictable social relationships to openly communicate these emotions, the more a speaker can borrow from a sense of safety in the social relationship to self-soothe and regulate both mind and body with the stress reduction offered by stimulation of the parasympathetic nervous system. This practice of expressing vulnerable emotions in warm and supportive relationships decreases stress in the mind and body to promote personal healing and recovery, while also reinforcing the connection in this particular social bond. With practice, these emotions can be regulated with greater personal control outside of healthy relationships, but first requires someone to experience the safe relational groundwork (ideally with primary caretakers) to create a baseline of optimal belief systems and behavior expectations for future experiences.[162]

---

162   Fosha D. (2009). Emotion and recognition at work: Energy, vitality, pleasure, truth, desire and the emergent phenomenology of transformational experience. In D. Fosha, D. J. Siegel and M. F. Solomon (Eds.), *The healing power of emotion: Affective neuroscience, development, clinical practice.* Chapter 7. New York: Norton. In press.

When I ask men about their experiences with this type of social safety in their childhood while growing up in my therapy practice, I tend to get two common answers. The first is an outright denial that there were ever emotional experiences of insecurity, fear, or shame while growing up. Even if a man *believes* they are reporting accurately, I know this is impossible because these emotions are a natural part of human life—and especially for kids who are constantly having new and stressful (at least for them) experiences due to the inherent novel nature of childhood. This tells me primary caretakers did *not* facilitate these important experiences and in fact, there was such an absence of them in daily family life that a "social taboo" formed around them—adding an extra layer of avoidance and resulting discomfort with vulnerability itself. The second most common answer that men provide to this line of questioning is that, "[they] couldn't talk to anybody about that stuff..."

This ability to express a full range of emotions—vulnerable ones included—along with intentional social application in response to adequate emotional attunement, is the missing piece that ties it all together. While human beings evolved to rely on emotion-focused communication for optimal function as fundamentally social animals, socialization processes teach boys to bury most of this primal wisdom below conscious awareness in a way that sets many up for social isolation, and resulting low of quality of life, not to mention various mental and physical health issues that have wreaked systemic havoc under the emerging pressures of modern society. It is time to reclaim and integrate humanity back into manhood with a full range of emotional intelligence.

CHAPTER 10: PUTTING IT ALL TOGETHER TO HEAL YOURSELF & SAVE THE WORLD

Emotions are essential for human beings because they provide the "missing link" to managing the dynamic balance between guiding choices in daily life with personal integrity and protecting connection in social relationships. Each emotion has developed along with the social needs of human beings to guide group problem solving in a way that promotes cohesion and connection, while also allowing space for personal advocacy.

Each emotion has its own "social action tendency"—its own evolutionary purpose and function that creates a change in physiology, behavior, experience, and communication to guide the dynamic balance between advocating for personal integrity and securing social connection.[163] It can seem like there are many different emotions—especially with limited exposure in the past—but in reality, there are only a handful of main emotional experiences that human beings have developed to meet social needs.[164]

These core emotions will be outlined here, along with their three basic functions. First, each emotion initially presents itself as an immediate and automatic judgment of the situation at hand. This happens automatically before conscious processing. Second, the meaning of the emotion is more consciously processed to inform new intentions for meeting personal needs.

163   Frijda, N. H. (1988). The laws of emotion. *American Psychologist*, 43, 349–358

164   Lowe, R., and Ziemke, T. (2011). The feeling of action tendencies: on the emotional regulation of goal-directed behavior. *Frontiers in psychology*, 2, 346. https://doi.org/10.3389/fpsyg.2011.00346

The third phase is social, where emotions are shared with others to meet needs for social connection and facilitate group problem solving.[165]

Emotion	Social Action Tendency	Personal Need
Anger	Assert self, set boundaries, even attack	Personal goal disrupted and motivation to engage
Shame/ Disgust	Distance self from another person as "outsider"	Personal drive to hide, but need *acceptance* for resolution
Anxiety/ Fear	Avoid people and/ or experiences as a perceived threat	Personal need of safety and security
Sadness	Slow down, withdrawal	Short-term decrease of motivation to reassess current inventory after personal loss of person or personal identity
Guilt	Problem solve to make amends	"Make right" after "doing wrong" by a tribe Member or Self
Joy/ Excitement/ Happiness	Move toward, continue current script	Increase motivation to continue engaging in current behavior that is satisfying personal goals

Oatley, K., and Johnson-Laird, P. N. (1987). **Towards a cognitive theory of emotions.** *Cognition and Emotion.* 1, 29–50.

---

165   Izard, C.E. (2010) The many meanings/aspects of emotion: definitions, functions, activation, and regulation. *Emotion Review,* 2, 363–370

Each of these emotions plays an important role in guiding human life by providing immediate feedback to each person in the form of personal judgment, insight into personal needs, and facilitating social needs. Altogether, they provide human beings with the tools required to live in community-based settings by utilizing collective strengths. The experience and expression of emotions is the "missing link" for adapting functionally to the dynamic needs of a chaotic natural world for many men.

Research from "appraisal theory"[166] has shown that "neural circuits" physically form in the brain to take into account and actively learn from ongoing personal experiences. These *neural circuits* include belief systems, emotions, thought patterns, and of course, behavioral habits that are encoded with each other to make it easier to reference them in the future, increasing likelihood of their functional use in the future. This allows people to track information constantly and automatically in the outside world for important indicators that are likely to reflect relevant knowledge gathered from previous experiences, then use this important data to guide daily decision-making in the present situation, as well as strategically plan for the future.

Our thought processes happen instantly below conscious awareness with "state dependent memory," where the most easily accessed memories from the past are always those that match the present emotional experience. This works very well to encourage ongoing survival since the behaviors and beliefs applied in previous experiences worked well enough in the past to get here today. However, repeatedly relying on that automatic survival mechanism does not leave much room for moving past those old defense mechanisms to break through limiting beliefs

166   Jamieson, J. P., Hangen, E. J., Lee, H. Y., and Yeager, D. S. (2018). Capitalizing on Appraisal Processes to Improve Affective Responses to Social Stress. *Emotion review : journal of the International Society for Research on Emotion*, *10*(1), 30–39.

and habits that have reinforced one's relative comfort zone. The circuits become more ingrained with repetition over time—a phenomenon called "Hebbian learning"[167]—and perhaps most widely recognized in mainstream psychology by the phrase, "what fires together wires together."

In this process, the mind automatically compares information from the present to the past, at which point an emotional reaction to the present situation automatically forms according to how this immediate experience fits within existing neural circuits.[168] This dynamic process facilitates how an individual learns to keep their personal needs in line with fluctuating contexts in a naturally chaotic world while living in a community-based setting with other human beings who have their own unique and fluctuating needs as well.

This is the tricky part because as we've discussed in detail, the social and cultural lessons around traditional manhood have made most men ashamed of this emotional wisdom. The social taboos surrounding emotions teach boys that showing emotions makes them look incompetent or even worse, weak, and dependent. These belief systems work together with the natural *social action tendency* for shame to hide the true self. This creates a compounding effect of self-numbing and avoidance in an attempt to avoid social rejection, which separates a person from consciously experiencing their emotions, blocks the development of authentic self-identity and associated personal needs from conscious awareness. That blockage, in turn, is also

167   Keysers, C., and Gazzola, V. (2014). Hebbian learning and predictive mirror neurons for actions, sensations, and emotions. *Philosophical transactions of the Royal Society of London. Series B, Biological sciences,* 369(1644), 20130175. https://doi.org/10.1098/rstb.2013.0175

168   Baumeister, R. F., Vohs, K. D., Nathan DeWall, C., and Zhang, L. (2007). How Emotion Shapes Behavior: Feedback, Anticipation, and Reflection, Rather Than Direct Causation. *Personality and Social Psychology Review,* 11(2), 167–203. https://doi.org/10.1177/1088868307301033

the primary barrier for meeting intimate social needs in our relationships with others.

This separates many men from their own humanity and self-identity, as well as from a healthy emotional life in their most intimate relationships. This not only harms an individual's own quality of life, but also stifles the emotional health of other people who share their social ecosystem. It is common for men and boys to have *significantly* less social training. As a result, men tend to have very limited practice with the important skill of identifying emotions in others—also called "emotional attunement" or "empathy." With this said, research has also shown that with a bit of motivation, *all human beings* can increase self-awareness of emotional experiences in themselves and others.[169]

An ability to use this emotional wisdom more fluently with self and others in times of stress creates mutual soothing — safe emotional processing that releases the bonding chemical oxytocin that naturally stimulates those natural healing processes associated with the parasympathetic nervous system.[170] Thus using our emotional wisdom turns off the body's stress response, thereby increasing immune response and returning our ability to critically think—all while building a sense of safety, trust, and understanding with the other people involved.

In the long-term, this natural cycle of emotional exchange in a relationship provides a safe place to grow and be nurtured for all parties involved. This experience of mutual soothing promotes trust and understanding for deeper intimacy and connection in

---

169   Ickes, W., Gesn, P.R., and Graham, T. (2000). Gender differences in empathic accuracy: Differential ability or differential motivation? *Personal Relationships*, 7, 95–109.
170   Coan, J.A., Schaefer, H.S., and Davidson, R.J. (2006). Lending a hand: Social regulation of the neural response to threat. *Psychological Science*, 17, 1032–1039.

personal relationships, where a *corrective emotional experience* occurs[171]—not only soothing emotional pain in the moment, but also giving the wounded party an opportunity to explore thoughts, feelings, behaviors, and belief systems outside of previously held limiting beliefs based on personal experiences up to that point.

This synergy creates a mutual flow where the energy flowing from one party into the other continues building onto itself, where it can then be used to increase the wisdom, proficiency, and connection between all participants.

While the benefits are certainly attractive, participation in these experiences will require men to develop the personal resilience to grow past the rigid belief systems of traditional manhood and learn new behaviors—especially as it relates to personal identity, social skills, and emotional awareness. Human beings have always been a social species and while short-term progress might be simpler with keeping an individual focus, long-term success and sustainability is dependent on our ability to meaningfully collaborate with community members, while keeping a healthy balance between personal needs and important social connections. As the old proverb goes, "If you want to go fast—go alone. If you want to go far—then go with others."

With an understanding of the importance of neural circuitry and using the right emotions at the right times, we can now look deeper at each individual core emotion.

---

171   Bridges M. R. (2006). Activating the corrective emotional experience. *Journal of clinical psychology*, 62(5), 551–568. https://doi.org/10.1002/jclp.20248

Anger

Anger tends to be the most widely accepted emotion for men and boys due to its perception of power, whereas the other emotions tend to be seen as a sign of weakness. It is common for men and boys to literally receive coaching and guidance to "use their anger" to access the motivational fuel inside of it. However, very rarely is the guidance coupled with advice on managing the problems associated with an overreliance on this aspect of it.

Anger is a commonly recognized emotion, at least in the United States. In a survey conducted in 1982, researchers found that, "most people report becoming mildly to moderately angry anywhere from several times a day to several times a week".[172] Anger also tends to grab attention, as described in the "anger superiority effect." The anger superiority effect is the tendency of people to recognize angry faces more quickly and accurately than other emotional expressions, because they are perceived as threatening, powerful, and dominant.[173]

Once activated, anger also colors a person's perceptions of judgment, guides decision-making and drives behavior until it has been regulated. Anger tends to influence people towards a general punitive/disciplinary stance,[174] a short-sighted optimism

---

172   Averill, J. R. (1982). *Anger and aggression: An essay on emotion.* New York: Springer-Verlag, p. 1146, see Chapter 19.

173   Clark, M. S., Pataki, S. P., and Carver, V. H. (1996). Some thoughts and findings on self-presentation of emotions in relationships. In G. J. O. Fletcher, and J. Fitness (Eds.), *Knowledge structures in close relationships: A social psychological approach* (pp. 247–274). Hillsdale, NJ: Lawrence Erlbaum Associates.

174   Goldberg, J. H., Lerner, J. S., and Tetlock, P. E. (1999). Rage and reason: the psychology of the intuitive prosecutor. *European Journal of Social Psychology,* 29(5-6), 781–795

about their own likelihood of success,[175] relative carelessness when it comes to strategy,[176] and eagerness to act.[177]

The beneficial purpose of anger is to provide the user with energy to act against others when there has been wrong-doing or injustice towards them. But even though anger provides the energy to advocate and set boundaries, the assumption of judgment/blame on the other party and lack of strategic focus are common ingredients that cause people to use anger improperly and ultimately get themselves into trouble, or just ignored. When we perceive anger from others, our social programming recognizes a threat inherent in an angry response from another person before it has even been consciously processed.

Due to the behavior expectations and belief systems around traditional manhood, it is common for boys and men to avoid most, if not all other emotions in favor of the relative safety that anger provides from more vulnerable emotions. Studies have shown a clear connection between the traditional manhood characteristics and an overreliance on anger in domestic disputes that lead to violence.[178] This is also in line with previous research on *attachment injuries* from childhood, which are also related to increased use of anger and dominance in adult relationships,

---

175   Lerner, J. S., Gonzalez, R. M., Small, D. A., and Fischhoff, B. (2003). Effects of fear and anger on perceived risks of terrorism: A national field experiment. *Psychological Science*, 14(2), 144–150.

176   Bodenhausen, G. V., Sheppard, L. A., and Kramer, G. P. (1994). Negative affect and social judgment: The differential impact of anger and sadness.[Journal. Special Issue: Affect in Social Judgments and Cognition]. *European Journal of Social Psychology*, 24(1), 45–62.

177   Harmon-Jones, E., Sigelman, J., Bohlig, A., and Harmon-Jones, C. (2003). Anger, coping, and frontal cortical activity: The effects of coping potential on anger-induced left frontal activity. *Cognition and Emotion*, 17(1), 1–24

178   Mahalik, J. R., Aldarondo, E., Gilbert-Gokhale, S., and Shore, E. (2005). The role of insecure attachment and gender role stress in predicting controlling behaviors in men who batter. *Journal of Interpersonal Violence*, 20(5), 617–631. doi:10.1177/0886260504269688

as well as an increased risk of domestic violence in romantic relationships.

Shame

Shame is an emotion that tells the host there is a risk of social rejection. Since human beings are such social creatures, the experience of shame is *very powerful*—bringing elevated attention to a situation that represents a risk to losing essential *love and belonging needs*. The risk of social abandonment is threatening to survival for human beings, so the emotional experience of shame automatically turns on the stress response of the mind and body— a.k.a. *"fight/flight/freeze."*

The *freeze response* associated with shame blocks conscious awareness of other emotions and by doing so, keeps them from being experienced consciously by the host, as well as expressed openly towards others. This serves an important survival function to protect essential *love and belonging needs* by blocking someone from behaving in a way that is likely to result in rejection or social shunning from loved ones and community members.

In order to avoid this potential rejection, a person depends on their relative comfort zone of personal experiences—even if it is self-loathing shame or being completely numb to emotions at all in order to avoid exploring viewpoints outside of the socially and culturally reinforced norms. This keeps the user trapped in a self-reinforced feedback loop of thoughts, feelings and behavior that protects them from potential social rejection, but at the cost of a personal belief that they are *indeed* unworthy of love and acceptance.

Shame creates a powerful inhibitory experience for all human beings to protect social belonging, but *especially* for men. This is due to the belief systems of traditional manhood that view emotional restriction as a sign of competence required for success and that outward expression of fear and pain is a sign of weakness. Even though there is a long social and cultural history that has shaped these belief systems, the basic social needs of human beings are even more primal and engrained on a biological level through our evolution as a species. The biochemical experience associated with emotions are *natural, healthy,* and *adaptive* for all human beings in their own specific contexts of personal experience, but the social and cultural expectations for men teach them that they resemble signs of lacking character and unworthiness of social acceptance.

This results in most men pushing down emotions (especially those outside of angry and happy), where they are repressed and then covered with *another* layer of this distinctly "male shame" associated with the gender role conflict inherent in the experience of most emotions. This *male shame* creates another layer of reinforcement for avoidance to protect perceived social position from being downgraded by mere affiliation with this social and cultural taboo. As a result of this dynamic layering uniquely characteristic of male shame, men are often faced with an uphill battle right off the starting block when it comes to increasing emotional intelligence. The *stress-inducing* biochemical experience of shame (freeze response) tends to be associated with most other emotions at the beginning of this exploratory process, and especially the more vulnerable ones. Sometimes this progresses to the point where any emotional experience is so uncomfortable and socially threatening, that they learn to push them out of conscious awareness entirely—compartmentalizing the experience of emotion entirely in a state of avoidance and numbing.

The open verbal expression of one's shame—however uncomfortable—is also a key to unlocking deeper connection and understanding with those around us. When expressed clearly in safe relationships—whether with a therapist, lover, or friend—the open expression of shame creates an experience of mutual soothing, allowing the parasympathetic nervous system to interrupt the sympathetic nervous system. The parasympathetic nervous system calms the body's stress response with a cascade of relaxing chemicals (oxytocin, serotonin, dopamine, etc.) that tells the user "your people will support you—you are worthy of love—you will be OK."

This social bonding process is very important for human beings, but men rarely learn to use the range of emotional intelligence required to facilitate these personal and social needs. This mostly unconscious lack of expression and ongoing repression creates an emotional pressure cooker that often results in anger, isolation, chronic self-neglect, and even dehumanization of self and other people.

The outward expression of *shame* is still not wise on the battlefield, but it is a natural emotional response for human beings when threatened with social rejection.[179] When shame cannot be expressed and processed with those who meet our *love and belonging needs* as designed to reinforce social safety/ belonging, it is turned inwards as *anxiety* where it becomes an obsessive focus on ruminating thoughts, or *depression* symptoms like "numbing" through avoidance until the holder develops a sense of "learned helplessness." If this goes on long enough, the repressed emotional pressure will develop into resentment until the anger is eventually expressed either outward towards someone else or inwardly as self-harming and self-sabotaging,

179   Steimer T. (2002). The biology of fear- and anxiety-related behaviors. *Dialogues in clinical neuroscience*, 4(3), 231–249. https://doi.org/10.31887/ DCNS.2002.4.3/tsteimer

rather than taking the level of social risk required to allow emotions adequate room for running their natural course and facilitating a healthy balance between self-advocacy and social connection.

Anxiety/Fear

Fear is another powerful emotion for human beings that is shared with most other animals.[180] This old and primal emotion provides personal insight into a potential threat of harm and in many ways, "anxiety" can be considered the younger sibling that provides a similar alert to a potential threat, just at a lower intensity. There is one notable difference between both of them however, in that *fear* is a more powerful response to a known external danger, whereas *anxiety* indicates more of a generalized response to an unknown threat or internal conflict.[181]

Fear and anxiety come with a biochemical reaction in the body that also trips the sympathetic nervous system, but unlike having a main tendency of "freezing" that is common with shame, fear/anxiety tend to come with two available adaptations based on a person's unique perspective. When the potential threat is far enough away not to represent an immediate danger of harm, a "freeze" response is more likely, versus when there is a more immediate risk of threat wherein the impulse to "flight" in order to avoid more actively takes priority.[182]

---

180   Panksepp J. *Affective neuroscience: The foundations of human and animal emotions.* New York: Oxford University Press; 1998.

181   Craig KJ., Brown KJ., Baum A. Environmental factors in the etiology of anxiety. In: Bloom FE, Kupfer DJ, eds. *Psychopharmacology: the Fourth Generation of Progress. New York, NY: Raven Press;* 1995:1325–1339.

182   Panksepp J. The psychoneurology of fear: evolutionary perspectives and the role of animal models in understanding human anxiety. In: Burrows GD, Roth M, Noyes Jr R, eds. *Handbook of Anxiety. Volume 3. The Neurobiology of Anxiety. Amsterdam, The Netherlands: Elsevier Science BV;* 1990:3–58.

Like shame, fear is another emotion that is designed to create social bonding and connection when shared with trusted loved ones through the stimulation of a "caretaking response."[183] If the people who make up our social connections are both emotionally equipped themselves and also intend to respect our integrity in the relationship, this *caretaking response* will naturally occur in the form of their desire to provide access for a warm and supportive social environment to safely process the emotional experience. This also requires someone who is able to withstand their own emotional discomfort, which tends to come with a set of barriers both unique and severely limiting for most men.

Sadness

Sadness is an emotion associated with loss—either losing a person, failure to achieve a personal goal or loss of a personal sense of control.[184] Loss is very difficult for all human beings since we are so social and therefore neurologically programmed for connection to other people and the shared meaning (social and cultural expectations) that binds a community together.

At the same time, the ability to recognize and gracefully accept the reality of change is very functional and adaptive in a chaotic natural world. In response to this important need for a more adaptive response to daily life stressors, the basis for *nonattachment* in Buddhism was formed. If it makes you feel better, this is not a simple task even for monks, who still spend their lives in monasteries committed to meditative practice to

---

183   Bowlby J. *A secure base: Parent-child attachment and healthy human development*. New York: Basic Books; 1988.
184   Ekman P. (1999). "Basic emotions," in *Handbook of Cognition and Emotion*, eds Dalgleish T., Power M. J. (New York, NY: Wiley;), 45–60.

get closer to their enlightenment, or "nirvana," that reflects a mastery of this "art of letting go."

The experience of sadness and loss creates what is almost like a short-term depression—where this temporary loss of energy once had for daily life *forces* someone to slow down and accept this loss as a realistic reflection of the present circumstances. Once this process of slowing down and acceptance of the loss has occurred, the sadness naturally resolves itself. In cases where sadness associated with loss and grief cannot be adequately expressed or personally experienced, it is repressed into the unconscious, where it continues to fester below the surface only to create further complications to both mental and physical health down the line.[185]

Sadness tends to get tricky for men not just because of the relatively weak and low energy state associated with it, but also because men are trained to identify so strongly with the ability to maximize production as part of the traditional provider role. As a result of this pressure to retain as much energy and time as possible for productivity, it rarely seems like a good idea to most men to allow space for sadness, which often blocks this emotion from running its natural course. The good news is like any other emotional experience, it comes with its own social and evolutionary functions of accepting a loss and once someone has had enough space to process the emotional experience, the sadness and its associated discomfort resolves itself.

Guilt

Guilt is like the younger sibling of shame. This emotion is an experience associated with the internal feedback that we have

185   Parkes C. M. (1998). Bereavement in adult life. *BMJ (Clinical research ed.)*, *316*(7134), 856–859. https://doi.org/10.1136/bmj.316.7134.856

behaved in a way that represents wrongdoing, but not to the degree of shame where this represents risk of social rejection.[186] Since guilt does not automatically reflect a perceived risk of social rejection that threatens basic needs, the body's acute stress response of the sympathetic nervous system does *not* get triggered by this emotion.

Whereas shame tells us that *we* are "wrong" or "unacceptable," the experience of *guilt* reflects social feedback that a specific *behavior/action* has not been acceptable.[187]

This is a situation where self-identity is *not* the central object of negative judgment, as with shame. Instead, the focus of *guilt* is on an action or behavior that impacted others negatively with the goal of correcting the problem with an apology or some other attempt to repair the relationship with prosocial behavior in order to actively correct the issue.[188]

Joy/Excitement/Happiness

Happiness is the emotion that teaches people how to access important resources. It tells us when something is pleasurable, which is marked in the brain as an experience that meets personal needs and wants. As a result, people learn that the pleasurable experience should be actively sought out in the future.[189] This emotion is largely facilitated by the "feel good" brain chemical dopamine, which is associated with meeting basic physical

186   Woien, S. L., Ernst, H. A. H., Patock-Peckham, J. A., and Nagoshi, C. T. (2003). Validation of the TOSCA to measure shame and guilt. *Personality and Individual Differences*, 35, 313 - 326
187   Tangney, J. P., Stuewig, J., and Mashek, D. J. (2007). Moral emotions and moral behavior, *Annual Review of Psychology*, 58: 345 - 372.
188   Tangney J. P., Wagner P. E., Gramzov R. (1989). *The Test of Self-Conscious Affect (TOSCA)*, Fairfax, George Mason University.
189   Smith, K.S., et al. (2010). Hedonic Hotspots: Generating Sensory Pleasure in the Brain. In: Kringelbach ML, Berridge KC, editors. *Pleasures of the Brain*. New York: Oxford University Press; pp. 27–49.

needs like food and shelter, as well as more abstract needs like creativity and meaningful social connection.[190] This emotion serves a very important function in the human learning process, where personal experience is reinforced through the pleasure associated with happiness, resulting in building an internally driven incentive for learning how to access experiences/ resources that must be essential for survival.

It is important to remember that as long as the pleasure centers of the brain are stimulated, the mind and body will learn to desire whatever experiences cause a dopamine rush. This is where addiction largely comes into play, where people become obsessed with consuming intoxicants or engaging in activities that provide these pleasure-inducing chemical reactions that the brain literally learns to hyper-focus on to avoid life stressors. Even if someone does not necessarily *want* to actively engage in addictive behavior, the disease of addiction is characterized by this constant desire to seek previously pleasurable experiences that got coded into the brain's "survival response" for coping with life stressors.[191]

The social function for *happiness* is to provide an experience of shared pleasure between community members. The shared experience of pleasure provides positive reinforcement for group membership and increases future likelihood of continuing to successfully cooperate in dynamic group problem solving.

Second only to anger, *happiness* is the other emotion that tends to be more acceptable for the belief systems and behavior expectations of traditional manhood—as long as one does not express *too much happiness*. When the intensity of happiness

---

190   Kringelbach ML. The Hedonic Brain: A Functional Neuroanatomy of Human Pleasure. In: Kringelbach ML, Berridge KC, editors. *Pleasures of the Brain*. Oxford: Oxford University Press; 2010. pp. 202–21.
191   Kringelbach, M. L., and Berridge, K. C. (2010). The functional neuroanatomy of pleasure and happiness. *Discovery medicine*, 9(49), 579–587.

reaches a certain limit, this creates *gender role conflict* with the expectations around emotional restriction and the avoidance of affection, which is a common combination that can be expected to be met with social policing in the form of homophobia and a decrease in social influence.

~ * ~

When a host is not willing to allow enough space for emotional experiences to take place and inform important decision-making, the emotions get pushed below the surface into the unconscious—where they only further complicate matters—rather than being used as intended by our social programming. There is only so much that can be pushed down until the pressure becomes too much to bear in the unconscious, at which point things begin to get messy. Studies looking directly at shame and guilt using brain imaging have shown that, regardless of gender, the expression of anger, hostility, irritability, resentment, suspiciousness, and paranoia are indicative of underlying shame below the surface.[192]   In fact, research has shown that when shame is pushed into the unconscious, the shame "bubbles up" into feelings of anger that are commonly redirected/displaced towards blaming other people and situations around them, i.e. projection.

This shows a clear link between shame and anger by noting that shame-prone people are not only likely to experience more anger, but are also more likely to manage their anger and resulting behavior in less adaptive ways, such as behaving with hostility and aggression towards others. That only further reinforces the feedback loop of limited self-awareness and social isolation. Unlike shame, guilt is not related to anger or hostility, but rather

---

192   Tangney JP: Shame and guilt in interpersonal relationships, in Self-Conscious Emotions, edited by Tangney JP, Fischer KW. New York, Guilford, 1995, pp 114–139

associated with an increased tendency to accept responsibility and engage in good faith.

All of these emotions have an adaptable function for the dynamic needs of human beings—allowing us to learn from personal experiences, meet basic needs, as well as manage the dynamic cooperation typical of a highly social species. Rational thought is also very important of course, but let's also remember the natural world is inherently chaotic, which limits the function of linear thought in daily life of the real world.

Human beings have always successfully managed this dynamic balance between personal needs and important relationships since our evolution as a social species—rising to the top of the food chain as dynamic group problem solving machines. Men have always played important roles as the primary providers of resources and physical protectors of loved ones and more vulnerable community members. Now as the world's population becomes a more interconnected community, communication of new information can now travel instantly from one previously disconnected and isolated corner of the globe to another, something that has only recently become possible after hundreds of thousands of years of human evolution.

Not only is the global population seven times denser than it was 120 years ago in 1900, but a compounding effect from the modern technological age has also forced the belief systems and behavior expectations of different social and cultural groups into greater proximity than human society has ever seen. The unfortunate result has been a dramatic increase in sociopolitical pressure between different social groups who were previously separated in more isolated communities. Now because of greater proximity, those groups are easily swept up in the automatic signals of a tribal nature saying, "*They* are dangerous! *They* need to change their ways to be the same as *ours! They* are the *problem!"*

On top of this naturally occurring tribal tension between previously isolated communities of the Old World, the corporate oligarchy in the United States alone spends roughly 250 billion dollars a year on marketing and advertising dollars to play off of these sources of fear and contention in order to promote panic spending and radicalize political ideology to control the public opinion, rather than solving the complicated issues at hand facing our community members.

Solving the problems of the world will take a global community with human beings who can act like we are a meaningful part of a cohesive group—committed to the dynamic and inclusive problem solving required in modern society to create sustainable solutions. Since the beginning of humankind, men have risen to the occasion as formidable providers of resources and protectors of our vulnerable community members. To continue fulfilling this destiny of our genetic programming as men, we must first heal our own unresolved wounds to get our *own* house in order. This requires building out a full range of emotional intelligence to backfill the social and emotional blind spots resulting from the fragmentation of our own human identity.

Once these new social and emotional skills are remastered, men can earn back the trust of community members by increasing mutual understanding and safety in relationships through mutual meaning-making in collaborative problem solving—just as the servant leaders whose shoulders we stand on today. This not only keeps men in balance with a meaningful source of purpose in daily life tasks, but also maintains healthy and trusting relationships with others in a way that optimizes productivity and unlocks the natural healing properties of the parasympathetic nervous system by engaging "as nature intended" for all community members involved.

Rebuilding Emotional Intelligence Exercise 1:

Now that all of the emotions have been explained in terms of their evolutionary purpose in terms of meeting personal needs, facilitating group cooperation and securing social needs, it's time to put this knowledge to use. The skills required to do so—that of "emotional intelligence"—is an important skill set that boys and men are rarely taught as part of the social and cultural expectations for everyday life.

This is largely a result of *gender role conflict* experienced by many men as they navigate modern society according to the behavior expectations and belief systems of traditional manhood, where social and cultural pressures are focused on limiting emotional expression, repressing vulnerable emotion, independence to the point of social isolation, devaluation of women, a preoccupation with winning in competition and/or collecting resources as a sign of "success," as well as an acceptance of violence to meet these ends. This leads many boys and men to miss out on developing a full range of *emotional intelligence* and rather, learn to rely heavily on either getting angry or avoiding emotions altogether. This leaves a *huge gap* when it comes to the required tools for meeting both personal and social needs as a human being in modern society who is also male.

Believe it or not, I have found in my practice that many men and boys cannot even feel their emotions at *all* due to such thorough social and cultural training to avoid them at *all* costs—or face the shame associated with social shunning and rejection. Remember we just discussed shame and how it effects the physical body by stimulating the *sympathetic nervous system* to generate a "freeze response" characteristic of the body's survival response?

For many men and boys, this personal experience of shame is pushed *deep* into the unconscious where it feels much less threatening in terms of immediate risk for social rejection, but with it, all the other emotions stay frozen underneath of this "invisible cloak"—along with fragments of self-identity and unmet personal needs that are buried along with it.

This unique experience of "masculine shame" acquired from the social and cultural pressures within traditional gender socialization blocks men from connecting with their own inner wisdom that is only possible with access to a full range of natural human emotions. Since the experience of shame is *powerful*—even capable of creating a sympathetic nervous system response—it literally buries other emotions underneath its weight. It is in this way that the experience of shame protects its host against risk of social rejection, while at the same time creating an unconscious prison that limits personal growth and meaningful connection to others.

Once men consciously work through any shame related to breaking the mold of traditional manhood, they can access the wisdom inside of a full range human emotion waiting underneath to identify personal unmet needs and effectively share them with others. It is through this authentic experience of self and others that people can do the much needed work of both integrating the unmet needs of true self, while also sharing mutual meaning-making with fellow community members. This is the true meaning of a "safe space," where all community members can honestly and respectfully encounter one another in order to promote mutual trust and understanding—allowing the very natural wisdom of each emotion's *social-action tendency* to play out as nature intended according to the *power of love*. Not only do these techniques serve to avoid oppression and violence, but they also maximize access to all of the gifts available from each community member for optimal problem solving.

1. There are four ways people commonly *avoid* authentic emotional experiences. It is important to first *recognize* these, then *redirect back to the emotional experience* so the user can have a chance to use the real emotional experiences as designed.

    a. *People Pleasing* – Telling others what they want to hear to avoid tension, rather than expressing personal thoughts and feelings.

    b. *Blaming* – Placing the focus of fault on other people rather than taking ownership of feelings and underlying personal needs.

    c. *Over-Rational* – Overfocusing on logic and linear thought, rather than expressing associated feelings and beliefs.

    d. *Irrelevant* – Redirecting focus towards unrelated or loosely associated topics, rather than a direct focus on content associated with emotional authenticity or tension.

2. Next time you take part in a tense emotional experience, take a moment to pay attention to your own habits when it comes to avoiding the uncomfortable emotion(s).

    a. It is common that people have one or two that we tend to use more than others.

3. Once you can identify your *own* common tactics of emotional avoidance, it is time to take this to the next level. Once you have practiced enough self-awareness to catch yourself using one of those tactics outlined in #1, use the following outline to record your experiences to start getting some practice—some "swings in the batting cage"—if you will. This is *no different* than athletes "watching the tape" as a part of the training process. And just like coach always said, "Perfect performance does not exist, but perfect practice *will* make you *better.*"

Date and Time	Who Were You With? Alone?	AVOIDANCE Tactic (rational, blaming, people pleasing, blaming, irrelevant)	FEELINGS	THOUGHTS	BEHAVIOR	HOW LONG?

Rebuilding Emotional Intelligence Exercise 1: Self Expression

This is a communication skill adopted from "Nonviolent Communication Theory"[193] called the "I-feel statement," which has been slightly modified to create space for greater social connection. It is *important to make sure these steps are followed in this order* so that the statement begins in "first person," also known as an "I-position." This is designed to minimize the defensiveness of the person who is listening by sharing personal emotional experience *first*, which gives the listener a chance to see the speaker as "human first," rather than feeling defensive or threatened by hearing the personal meaning first.

NOTE—If the speaker does not share their feelings first and rather, shares the "personal meaning" characterized by #3 first, this will come off as the speaker making assumptions about the other party and their intentions—often resulting in defensiveness by the other party. If the speaker shares their "personal wants/needs" characterized by #4 first, then they will come off as demanding and critical.

1. "I feel _____
   _____."

   (name emotional experience[s])

2. "When _____
   _____."

   (describe the circumstances/context)

---

193   Rosenberg, M. B. (1999). Nonviolent communication: A language of compassion. Encinitas, CA: PuddleDancer Press.

3. "Because _____

_____."

(describe personal meaning)

4. "I need _____

_____."

(wants/needs that emotion is advising)

Once we know they have all the information they need, we can listen to their response to show to us how much they are ready to help us meet our needs, versus how much they will maintain a focus on their own needs.

4 Core Skills for Emotional Intelligence

Emotional intelligence is broken down into four main areas of functioning, with two based on awareness/management of self and the other two based on awareness/management of others in social relationships.

	What I See	What I Do
Personal Knowledge	*Self-Awareness*	*Self-Management*
Social Knowledge	*Social Awareness*	*Social Management*

Self-Awareness (see exercise #1)

Self-awareness is the foundation for personal influence. Once we are attuned to our own emotions in play at any given moment, these point to the direction of our personal needs, as well as provide the energy to get there. This is essential for self-care and healthy self-advocacy because it involves an understanding of *thoughts and feelings relative to a given situation*, which points to unmet personal needs.

It is *important* to be mindful about monitoring *self-awareness* because when we lose track, it is much easier to get drawn off course by an emotional reaction and as a result, make incorrect assumptions about ourselves relative to other people. This is most likely to occur when under stress in a common phenomenon aptly named a "cognitive error."[194] These *cognitive errors* create misjudgment in processing—like "all or nothing thinking" (perceiving extremes rather than a realistic middle ground), "catastrophizing" (assuming a worst-case scenario), or "personalizing" (taking responsibility for something that isn't your fault).

These *cognitive errors* are most likely to reflect belief systems learned in childhood either directly or indirectly through personal experiences. As discussed earlier, defensive reactions effectively used to survive threatening experiences get encoded by the brain as *survival scripts* for future use in times of stress. This means that the more stress someone experiences in the present, the more likely they are to take mental shortcuts (also called "regress") in defensive posturing, which is likely to produce the same *cognitive errors* that have always been

---

194   Rnic, K., Dozois, D. J., and Martin, R. A. (2016). Cognitive Distortions, Humor Styles, and Depression. *Europe's journal of psychology*, 12(3), 348–362. https://doi.org/10.5964/ejop.v12i3.1118

used as mental shortcuts to get by in times of stress.[195] This is especially common when someone is coming from a position of *social privilege* because their leveraged social location becomes a kind of "bubble"—insulated from realistic perspective taking by an overreliance on use of personal influence to remain relevant, rather than considering more humility, adaptation and collaboration for process improvement.

Self-Management

This is the ability to influence our mind, body, and immediate physical space to meet personal wants and needs.

Self-management includes the ability to control our behavior when we are having strong emotional experiences resulting in physical tension—also called "self-regulation." Studies have shown clear evidence of the connections between body and mind, so rather than letting those internal systems "run the show," it is up to *each individual* to reclaim the intentional use of these self-regulatory systems. There are many available skills for *self-management*, but we will focus on self-expression and self-advocacy in this book.

The development of personal awareness around how to use emotional experiences is an essential skill for identifying personal needs, growing past old limits, and learning to speak up for one's personal needs in a way that makes others *want* to listen. It is important to note that as a speaker develops their abilities to clearly express thoughts, feelings, and intentions, this will allow other people to understand their message more clearly and have a chance to respond with greater clarity themselves.

---

195   Ward, T., Keown, K., and Gannon, T. A. (2007). Cognitive distortions as belief, value, and action judgements. In Gannon, T. A., Ward, T., Beech, A. R., and Fisher, D. (Eds), *Aggressive offenders' cognition: Theory research and practice (pp. 53-70)*. Chichester, UK: John Wiley.

In order to support the reader in completing their due diligence for managing this dynamic, we will provide some communication skills using techniques from "Nonviolent Communication," as proposed by studies from evidence-based research in the fields of communication theory and conflict resolution.

Social Awareness

Social awareness is the practice of paying attention to others' emotions based on *what* they are saying and *how* they are saying it. The fields of behavioral science, psychology, and communication theory have provided a wealth of research that supports the importance of not only what is *literally* stated, but *also* the "nonverbal communication"—tone, timbre, volume, rate of speech, posture, and context.[196]

Once we learn to understand those aspects of communication, we can assess incoming communication for important insights that are essential for maintaining connection and trust with others, and especially in social spaces characterized by high levels of emotion or collaborative problem solving. After someone learns how to track this social information, we can move towards responding in a way that helps other people know we understand their position enough to be considered "on the same team," and therefore safe for ongoing meaningful connection.

---

196   Denham, M. A., and Onwuegbuzie, A. J. (2013). Beyond Words: Using Nonverbal Communication Data in Research to Enhance Thick Description and Interpretation. *International Journal of Qualitative Methods*, 670–696. https://doi.org/10.1177/160940691301200137

Social Management

Social management is where all of these skills come together by using the emotions of self and others in order to communicate more effectively, build trust, and develop collaborative efforts that promote use of available resources while also protecting group cohesion and safety. The technique that will be shared in this book has been named "Emotional Dialogue," a relatively simple technique that allows a speaker to communicate with another person in a way that promotes trust, understanding, and respect for optimal group cohesion. This same technique also releases the listener from the pressure of being an "expert" and rather, allows space for their authentic self to be present and available to appreciate the speaker with less judgment and more unconditional support.

Once a user has learned to interact with other people in this way, the people who the user encounters are more likely to experience a sense of personal understanding and respect for their unique position that can also be called "compassion" or "empathy." From here, each party is *much* more likely to practice flexibility in collaborative problem solving—even when a difference of personal belief systems arises—because all community members can navigate this emotional tension in a way that maintains respect and trust with mutual understanding. In turn, this promotes a personal sense of safety for all parties involved, allows a group to bring all the available resources to bear for dynamic group problem solving and protects, and even reinforces, personal relationships through the process of effective collaboration.

Rebuilding Emotional Intelligence Exercise 2: Supportive Listening

This is the response portion of the "Emotional Dialogue" skill set. Just like you want to be heard and understood when sharing personal thoughts and feelings, let's make sure you can do the same. This skill is designed to create a sense of safety and reliability through unconditional acceptance and non-judgment towards the speaker who is sharing their personal thoughts/feelings. To the degree that this sense of acceptance is communicated, the speaker will feel heard and validated, which creates an environment primed for more information sharing and improved problem solving, as well as healthy and sustainable connection that provides ongoing opportunity for mutual healing, recovery, and empowerment of "both sides" within the security of this safe relationship firmly established.

This is what a loved one *wants* when they say, "You are not *hearing* me! I just want you to *listen* to me!"

1. Validate – Reply back with a short summary to be clear that message received.

"If I'm hearing you correctly, (insert summary here) _____."

> a. This involves using a skill called "tracking" from *active listening,* where the listener attends to what the other person is saying and when they are done, *summarizes* what has been heard back to the speaker. Be *brief,* but make sure to name a few *specific* items the speaker expressed directly. (e.g., "I understand/hear you" is too *general* and will come off as dismissive.)

2. Say "*Thank You*" – It's a good idea to **express appreciation for their sharing** because:

> a.   Reminds the listener to *slow down* and *respond*, rather than *react* in a way that will sound defensive, critical, or combative.

> b.   This keeps the speaker more open and comfortable in an emotional space that feels vulnerable. This makes the speaker more likely to continue expressing their personal thoughts and feelings because the speaker will experience the listener as eager and willing to hear what the speaker is saying, rather than just waiting for their turn to speak.

3. Share Empathy – *Clearly* **share what you guess *their* emotional experience to be:**

"Wow/jeez/gosh/etc., that sounds [insert emotion word(s) here] _____ ."

> a.   This does **NOT** involve coming up with solutions, relating the event to personal experiences, or even apologizing. There might be a time for these approaches *after* an active invitation by the speaker, but now is *not* the time! Once the speaker feels heard and understood by the listener, their parasympathetic nervous system will stimulate a soothing response resulting in their feeling safer, at which point the speaker can *ask/solicit* feedback from the listener when *they* are ready. Even though this does not feel natural to most people and men tend to be more likely to offer advice, it is very important that the listener *waits* for this request so that the speaker feels

empowered, rather than being seen as someone who can't solve their own problems.

b.   This **DOES** show that the listener is willing to consider "what it is like to walk a mile in their shoes," and this creates a sense of "same team" where both parties feel safe for ongoing information sharing that in turn allows *further* connection and trust in helpful applications for leadership and intimacy alike.

c.   This **DOES** show that you RESPECT them enough to give them room to have their *own* experience, then **trust they will ask for help or advice** *themselves* **if/when** *they* **are ready.**

AUTHOR BIO

Logan Cohen is a professional therapist, a clinical supervisor for the American Association of Marriage & Family Therapy, and a serial entrepreneur in Charlotte, North Carolina. He lives with his wife, their 6-year-old son, identical twin daughters and their three dogs. Despite the enjoyment of early professional success and the beautiful gifts of a healthy and loving family, this was not always the author's life trajectory.

Logan had painful experiences with childhood abuse and like most boys, he was taught to keep personal problems private and to fight through discomfort silently in order to be seen as "strong and successful." Also similar to many other young men, this came at the cost of his own mental health. After being diagnosed with ADHD as a young boy and battling addiction as a young man to cope with the unresolved wounds, Logan was headed for the same pitfalls that claim the lives of many men in their prime and through midlife today.

It wasn't all dark and gloomy, though. In addition to the difficult family experiences as a boy, there was also an extended network of grandparents available to pass on the wisdom of a rich family history. Perhaps the most central of these figures early on for Logan was his "Grandpa Sam," a Holocaust survivor who was rescued from the Auschwitz Concentration Camp by Oscar Schindler. Logan had the pleasure of growing up only a few doors away from Sam and between the captivating stories of surviving World War II and meeting immediate safety needs, Sam's home became a favorite location for Logan as he sought refuge from the chaotic dynamics of his own childhood home. Even though Logan did not appreciate the weight and depth of these life experiences in his earlier years, themes of personal survival and community resilience became a central source of influence throughout the author's life as an adult.

After completing an undergraduate degree at the University of Georgia, Logan answered a call to adventure as a counselor and teacher with at-risk youth in a wilderness-based correctional facility located in the foothills of the Appalachian Mountains for three years. It was there in this spartan natural setting, with no electricity and temporary housing built with hand tools, that Logan got sober from his addiction, discovered his own purpose as a natural healer and observed the medicinal forces of intentional community living. After completing what he calls his "second coming of age" in the Appalachian wilderness, Logan went back to graduate school at Lewis & Clark College for additional training in Counseling Psychology with a goal of understanding and recreating these restorative dynamics in a modern therapeutic setting. Today Logan is a regional leader in the professional academic community, where he provides ongoing clinical training to other mental health professionals and healthcare workers around cultural competency with men, trauma recovery and violence prevention using evidence-based models.

Based on his own life experiences and healing journey, Logan decided to devote his work to serving those who are going through their own difficult life transitions by empowering them to break through barriers left from old unresolved wounds, heal themselves, and realign with their life's purpose for creating shared meaning with their own gifts as a valued community member.

Printed in the USA
CPSIA information can be obtained
at www.ICGtesting.com
LVHW010512070923
757436LV00005B/11